Nigeria's un-Civil WAR

Nigeria's un—Civil WAR

Memories of a Biafran Child

Philip Effiong

First published in Great Britain in 2023 by
Pen & Sword History
An imprint of
Pen & Sword Books Ltd
Yorkshire – Philadelphia
Copyright © Philip Effiong 2023
ISBN 9781399066013

The right of Philip Effiong to be identified as Author of this work has been asserted by him in accordance with the Copyright, Designs and Patents Act 1988.

A CIP catalogue record for this book is available from the British Library.

All rights reserved. No part of this book may be reproduced or transmitted in any form or by any means, electronic or mechanical including photocopying, recording or by any information storage and retrieval system, without permission from the Publisher in writing.

Set in Adobe Caslon Pro 13/17
Cover image Imaeyen Effiong
Printed and bound in the UK by CPI Group (UK) Ltd.,
Croydon. CR0 4YY

Pen & Sword Books Limited incorporates the imprints of Atlas, Archaeology, Aviation, Discovery, Family History, Fiction, History, Maritime, Military, Military Classics, Politics, Select, Transport, True Crime, Air World, Frontline Publishing, Leo Cooper, Remember When, Seaforth Publishing, The Praetorian Press, Wharncliffe Local History, Wharncliffe Transport, Wharncliffe True Crime and White Owl.

For a complete list of Pen & Sword titles please contact
PEN & SWORD BOOKS LIMITED
47 Church Street, Barnsley, South Yorkshire, S70 2AS, England
E-mail: enquiries@pen-and-sword.co.uk
Website: www.pen-and-sword.co.uk
Or
PEN AND SWORD BOOKS
1950 Lawrence Rd, Havertown, PA 19083, USA
E-mail: Uspen-and-sword@casematepublishers.com
Website: www.penandswordbooks.com

'Philip recounts the events with the directness of the child from whose memory they are retrieved. He avoids the adult filter that might mould them to fit a stereotype of virtue or villainy. This honest talking and writing about experiences of those frightful years inevitably unearths pain, contradictory points of view, preconceptions and misconceptions. However, this may be the surest way that we have to confront our transgenerational national trauma. Confront it we must, and in doing so we may be able to hear each others' pain and fears. Then, perhaps tentatively, find a path on which to take our next steps without once again 'setting fire to our home'. I find this book a homage to our past, and a gift to our future.'
— Babajide Adeniyi-Jones

'It is a fresh insight into this timeless story. I particularly enjoyed the way the book frames the easy friendships amongst the children against the casual brutality raging in the adult world above them. I don't think any account of the Biafra war can be more front row, up close and personal than this.'
— Dele Ogun

Contents

Dedication	7
Author's Note	9
Prologue	14
Chapter 1: AN Barracks, where creation began	16
Chapter 2: View from the mountain and the valley	32
Chapter 3: The rising sun that kept rising	43
Chapter 4: Red skies, red rain	58
Chapter 5: The Promised Land, without milk or honey	76
Chapter 6: Banished from our blue paradise	89
Chapter 7: Sleepwalking to the beat	111
Chapter 8: The future was around us, bright and desolate	130
Chapter 9: The grass on which the elephants wrestled	147
Chapter 10: The Biafran scar	170
Epilogue	173
Appendix: Index of Biafran War Songs	178
Acknowledgements	187

Dedication

This book is for –

My father, Philip Efiong Sr, an eternal embodiment of the Biafran spirit, in memory.

My mother, Josephine Efiong, without whom we would not have survived the war and post-war era.

My big brother, Valentine, who departed unexpectedly in August 2021, in memory.

My aunt and second mother, Mama Nkechi, an angel in every sense of the word.

My wife, Chinwe, to whom I am immensely thankful for love and patience unsurpassed.

My daughters Imaeyen, Amaeka and Idara, whose utmost devotion brings me supreme joy and a reason to press on.

My son Noah, for his gentleness and creativity.

All Biafran soldiers, living or dead, for relentless determination and courage.

All innocent victims, on both sides, whose blood will never dry.

'… it is only the story [that] can continue beyond the war and the warrior. It is the story that outlives the sound of war-drums and the exploits of brave fighters. It is the story…that saves our progeny from blundering like blind beggars into the spikes of the cactus fence. The story is our escort; without it we are blind.'
– Chinua Achebe, *Anthills of the Savannah*, 1987

'This is why I weep and my eyes overflow with tears. No one is near to comfort me, no one to restore my spirit. My children are destitute because the enemy has prevailed.'
– Lamentations 1:16

Author's note
Recasting Biafra and the Biafran child

This is not *the* Biafran story. This is *my* Biafran story. It is not entirely about airstrikes, starvation, death, suffering, displacement and refugees. Though these problems were rampant in Biafra, the nation was an embodiment of many more elements that are just as important as the desolation and hysteria. To constantly portray Biafra as an aberration to nationhood, which is the preferred narrative, is not only false but an insult to the resourcefulness of a people whose astronomical achievements in science, technology, management and security – under the most dreadful circumstances – remains unparalleled in modern Africa and most parts of the world. Sadly, even former Biafrans and self-styled pro-Biafrans often disperse this decadent image.

Like any nation, Biafra had a government, administrative units, an army, a navy, an air force, a police force, a flag, an anthem and a currency. Biafra provided a measure of education and healthcare, and issued passports and postage stamps to its citizens. Like any regime, institution, or family, Biafra had hierarchical formations that established power and authority based on status and position. Like people everywhere, Biafrans found time to laugh, play, pray, work, create, sing, dance, fall in love, make love, marry, travel and have children.

This is not to trivialize the anguish that Biafra had to contend with each day or the fact that every Biafran life was adversely altered, be it socially, economically, or emotionally. Privilege didn't immunize anyone against the real and unpredictable threats that the war served generously, to say nothing of the victimizations that continued many years after the onslaught. Even the Biafran leader lost his brother to the war. I lost my aunt, my younger cousin and grandfather, besides having our family home blown to bits at Ikot Ekpene. All Biafran youths lost at least three years of regular education, with many having to contend with irregular schooling patterns even before the war began. I ended up skipping, or partially completing, preschool to elementary four, which was about four years of inconsistent formal education from ages five to nine. The experience was loaded with more than enough tragedy to go around at various degrees of intensity, from individual to individual, family to family, and community to community. Notwithstanding this fact, it is unconscionable to define Biafra as a disaster embraced by aimless, delusional individuals crippled by fear, disease, dejection, scarcity, and abandonment. Many died in Biafra, but many were protected. Many were exposed to danger, but many were saved. Many starved, lost their homes and fell sick. But many were fed, re-accommodated and healed. Many were displaced and lost their families, but many were also given a new lease on life, even if it meant being relocated to a friendly, neighbouring country. It is all thanks to the determination, efficiency, ingenuity and courage of the people and their helpers. This other Biafra needs to be rediscovered, recognized and proclaimed. Not to do so would discredit the steadfastness and industry of the people. Not to do so would disregard the self-sacrificial principles that sustained the people. This other Biafra is to be celebrated; it is not to be mourned.

In this story I celebrate Biafra blatantly and unapologetically.

Ages five to nine are the most memorable years of my life. The Nigeria-Biafra war raged, preceded by pre-war disruptions that had already taken their toll on my family. I was a loyal Biafran. The war has always been described as *civil* despite its attainment of high levels of *un-civility*. The memories are vivid and therefore captivating. Because they are vivid, they remain alive in the most private and desperate regions of my psyche. I remember, even if some of my recollections are purer than others.

Biafra gave birth to children who navigated all sorts of obstacles, but they all remain her children without prejudice or preference. I am one of those children. To define the Biafran child from a rigid standpoint is not only stereotypical but cites the effects of war as predictable, fixed, and purely tangible. I am therefore not symbolic of the Biafran child. Nobody is.

Struggle and suffering are relative. They present different dimensions and perspectives with some being harsher than others. But all are relevant when contemplating the experiences that produced the Biafran child. Privilege is equally relative but as wars progress the line is easily blurred between the privileged and underprivileged, especially on the losing side. It becomes obvious that a bomb is not selective when it is dropped and that having the purchasing power is useless when the item to be purchased does not exist.

This is not a story about war per se, but a story that shows war to be inharmonious with human nature. It is therefore a story about the hunger for normalcy in the face of tremendous chaos, anxiety and devastation. In some ways it is also a story about pretence, about the depiction of a lifestyle that could have been but wasn't.

As in all wars, the players on both sides of the Nigeria-Biafra

War have refused to accept guilt, including me. This is not about pointing fingers and laying blame; it is not about rationalizing or accusing; it is not about defining heroes and unveiling cowards. I am not at all preoccupied with assessing the motives of the war, examining structures built to meet the war effort, evaluating battle strategies, or determining winners and losers. This is a child's story; it is innocently incapable of doing more than saying, 'this is what I saw; this is how I saw it; this is what I remember; this is what I thought, and this is how I felt'.

That the pictures here are filtered through the mind of a child does not exclude the possibility of an adult perspective in certain areas; I would be lying if I say this has not happened. War, after all, has the power to steal childhood. Some of what is expressed here is therefore the outcome of innocence lost then, not just in adulthood. This is an essential part of the story – the rendition of adulterated innocence, of innocence steeped in a cesspool that didn't have to be. Yet, it is the innocence and not the cesspool that has prevailed, for a child is defined by innocence and not the aimless spread of rot. During the war, I was conscious of the irrationalities that plagued my world. They may have tainted my perceptions of existence, but they failed to steal all my innocence.

In the end, I grew faster than I should have and, in songs and stories, interpreted violence as an ironic but necessary instrument of survival. Perhaps I didn't fully understand how this survival had been fiercely contested on an altar where blood flowed richly. I didn't understand how the process called for the sacrifice of all that was supposed to be human. But I understood that the preservation of dignity took precedence over life lived in humiliation and, again, songs and stories underscored this message. They drew a clear line between the good that we were required to embrace and the evil that we were warned to reject, between the heroes that shielded us and the intruding villains that were determined to break through that protection.

Throughout the war, therefore, my ability to retain youthful laughter and contentment had more to do with the portrayal of Biafra as a carefully assembled and righteous utopia, and less to do with the relative *luxury* that I enjoyed. Because this image has never been completely lost, despite how much it has been tampered with, its power continues to provide a reason to rejoice and have faith in possibilities that defy reason. Whatever the cesspool, whatever the dark tunnel, Biafra always promised a light at the unpredictable end of its saga, though it flickered fiercely because its flame was naked and raw. But it never went out.

I am not *every* Biafran child; no one can lay claim to that status. However, like all other Biafran children, I battled with the awareness that stability was lost to chaos. I remain, therefore, a valid and proud product of Biafra, and one of her many legitimate children. Like the mother that would not deny any of her children, regardless of their strengths, weaknesses, and unequal stages of development, Biafra will not deny me. I am not *the* Biafran Child. I am *a* Biafran child, *a* Biafran boy. For this reason, I will always carry the Biafran *passport*, even if only in spirit. And, like every story driven by the Biafran spirit, this is a story of victory without any shame or regret.

Prologue

Interruption

The peace had been desecrated. I knew because people spoke in low tones and laughter seemed to dry up where it once flourished. My father was more absent from the house and extra effort was made to keep us indoors.

Outside, everything seemed to unfold without grace or colour, even the harmattan leaves were more dried-up and skeletal than usual. The sun still shone but didn't smile and was therefore helpless against dreary clouds; it was as if the latter could tell that the worst was yet to come. Change should not have been bad, but this one was heavy and stubborn.

Months later I learned about the 15 January 1966 coup d'état.

But there was still room for laughter, childhood curiosity and mischief. Life thus went on without grief and 34 AN Barracks, with its simple furnishings and vast outdoor space, remained serene and snug, even though my father was no longer Director of Ordnance. Family outings resumed with the climax being Angela's birthday party at State House where Major General Johnson Umunnakwe Aguiyi-Ironsi loomed large as first military head of state. He was even larger when he showed up briefly, said something to the celebrant, patted her fondly and disappeared. I secretly pouted after Angela was awarded a small prize in one of those now-obscure party games that I thought I should have won. But it was her party, and she was the head of state's daughter.

The calm was short-lived, replaced by chaos explained in anxious whispers. The second coup of 29 July 1966 was much bloodier than the first and forced us out of 34 AN Barracks, which had sheltered my beginnings. Even worse, we were without the comfort and reassurance of my father's presence, and nobody seemed to know where he was.

From his base as Acting Commander of the First Brigade at Kaduna, he had barely escaped the wrath of the insurgents. We all grieved, but it was my mother who grieved the loudest. My mother's anguish was understandable. She and my father were very close; they were openly romantic and more like boyfriend and girlfriend than they were husband and wife. She fondly called him *eyeneka*, though it sounded like *nyeka*, which means brother in Ibibio, our language. He called her Josey, short for Josephine.

Chapter 1

AN Barracks, where creation began

I remember growing up in Lagos, which used to be Nigeria's capital city. Our home was at 34 AN Barracks in Yaba. Life was bright and simple, though my memories are slightly dull and somewhat jagged around the edges. I was four years old and then five. They tell me that life actually started for me in Kaduna, but I have failed in every attempt to recreate it, not even the blurry details. I was named Philip after my father, which has raised questions since I am his third son and not his first. I have also been told that my full name is Philip-Norbert though Norbert has long been lost to disuse.

Things were basic but adequate. Wooden seats fitted with square cushions – trendy back then – were arranged around a centre wooden table in our living room. Most of our furniture matched this simplicity, except for my mother's washing machine, truly a wonder for its time. It was, however, quite basic and didn't nearly flaunt the type of sophistication that comes with modern washing machines. It may also have been used for only certain fabrics and garments since most of our clothing were handwashed. At one corner of the living room was a small black television. A transparent, rainbow-colored, plastic sheet was draped over the screen to simulate colour, though it was distorted and amusing. Like the television, the telephone was black and rested on a small table, making its own unique contribution to the overall modest touch of modernity. I kept away from the telephone as I was required to; it was one of those gadgets that we children were banned from using. Only my mother and father could touch and use it.

The house was the standard for Lieutenant Colonels, with three bedrooms and a full bathroom upstairs, a toilet squeezed somewhere beneath the staircase, and abundant outdoor space. Because Nigeria's army didn't have too many officers back then, accommodation was sufficient and we were content – me, my two older brothers and two older sisters. I remained the youngest until Francis was born a year before we had to move out of AN Barracks. Soon after my mother gave birth, my father took us to the military hospital to see who would eventually turn out to be the only thumb-sucking, left-handed child in the family. We weren't allowed into the hospital room for whatever reason and I remember how we viewed things through a wide glass window as my mother held up the new arrival for us to see.

"His head looks like a light bulb," Charles, my immediate older brother, would later observe.

Our home was full of activity. Besides military aides who did domestic work, relatives came and went, like my father's immediate younger half-brother, Etim, who was kind, playful, and gave me some of my first lessons in the Ibibio language. My father's older brother, whom we called Etok á Papa, Small or Lesser Father, was also a familiar face. He was small or lesser in deference to his father, my grandfather, who was the supreme patriarch of our family. He was cheerful and spent time telling us folktales and teaching us Ibibio songs. A Second World War veteran, he was small in stature and looked nothing like my father, though he was my father's only sibling from his mother; the rest were from their father's other three wives. We called my father's mother, Ekamba Mma, Grandmother. Once she arrived, she took on the role of supreme disciplinarian, which we found quite hilarious. Later, I learned that she had raised me in my early years when my father went off to his several officer-training courses, taking my mother with him. But she didn't only show up when my father was away on training. She visited regularly and became an intimate part of our lives. Whenever she raised her voice or picked up a cane to mete out punishment for any of our several pranks, we took to our heels and were entertained by her efforts at catching up with us.

Next to Grandmother and my mother, our eldest, Rosalyn, assumed the role of disciplinarian and took steps to put us back on the right track when she thought we went astray. Although harmony mostly reigned among us, we sometimes disagreed. Occasional scraps between Mercy and Valentine, the second and third, were therefore not unusual, though quite legendary. Although Charles was barely two years older than me, I tried not to make him angry. He was quite the gladiator while I was notoriously gutless. Valentine, the eldest boy, had set himself apart as a gifted artist from a young age. Though harmless and full of laughter, his spirited craving for adventure and mischief sometimes landed him in trouble; like the day he stepped on a piece of broken glass. It tore into the flesh under his foot and caused part of the skin to dangle like a piece of thin cloth. I'm not sure what he tried to accomplish by washing the gash with the tap water behind the house, which only created a pool of red in the cement sink. Because my parents were not at home, our faithful and good-humoured cook, Eyo, finally took Valentine to the hospital, ferrying him on the crossbar of his black bicycle.

Life was bright, simple and sufficient. But sometimes it was more, like the time a white man visited and delivered a large box of green apples. It must have been a large box indeed because it took my mother a fairly long time to unpack and store them. In her usual way, she ended up giving most of the apples away and for that reason they didn't last long.

There weren't many instances of anxiety, but they did exist, like the day during my preschool days when I got too bored with being at home all by myself. I put on my sandals and headed out of the house; my destination was my mother's sewing shop, though I didn't know where it was. But I kept on walking. I arrived at the gate leading into the Barracks and was recognized by the guards. I knew that my adventure had ended, but it wasn't because the guards wouldn't let me through. It was because I feared the massive traffic jam on the other side of the gate. In a matter of minutes, one of the guards hauled me on to the crossbar of his bicycle and ferried me home.

Amusement and leisure were as simple and exhilarating as everything else. AN Barracks was a community of close friendships, some closer than others. We visited everyone and everyone visited us, but it was with the Trimnells that we exchanged the most visits. Lieutenant Colonel Trimnell, like my mother, was part British and from Ashaka in today's Delta State. His Yoruba wife, six children, and one cousin occupied a home like ours. Titi, the youngest of the Trimnell children, was mine, and at four or five I may have experienced the innocent and wishy-washy impulses of a harmless crush. We did little more than play games, but sometimes we held hands affectionately as if to reassure ourselves that we were sufficient for each other. When we became more adventurous and pecked each other on the lips, we didn't realize that we were being peeped at by our older brothers and sisters. Not until they teased us, exposing what we thought was our secret.

Besides neighbourly games and laughter, there were those netball matches that my mother participated in, which involved semi-serious competitions between officers' wives. They were hardly as exciting as our occasional trips to Bar Beach on Victoria Island, which had been spewed out by the Atlantic Ocean. Tarkwa Bay, partly decorated with an impressive thick collection of foliage and palm trees, was the other huge mass of water that lured us from home and, because it sits on an island near Lagos, required a boat ride to get there. The Trimnells were our usual companions on those exciting outings to the beach, during which we splashed in the water, ran around, played games, drank soft drinks, and snacked on coconuts and biscuits. I didn't know how to swim and therefore wasn't among those who ventured into the deeper water. I was about twelve years old when I eventually learned how to swim.

Sometimes we entertained at home in the form of a birthday party for a child or adult. Valentine and I shared the same birthday despite a three-year age difference and this unusual coincidence on 5 November was marked as a marvel worthy of uninterrupted celebration. We therefore enjoyed more birthday parties than anyone else, which I relished despite the veiled favouritism. Another marvel was Mercy's birthday, which is on 25 December. Though she should have received two gifts on this special day, she never did.

And then there were those long vacation road trips to Ikot Ekpene in the southeast, where my father's parents and extended family lived, and to Zaria in the north, where my mother's mother lived, also with family members. She was a very successful landlady and single parent (widow) whom we simply called Mama. While Ikot Ekpene was where my father had been partially raised, Zaria was my mother's birthplace and where my parents had met after my father was posted there on military assignment. Our visits to Ikot Ekpene and Zaria, besides offering a break from the hustle and bustle of Lagos, allowed us to be supremely pampered by our grandparents. We enjoyed maximum hospitality, which also meant being served a daily assortment of delicious meals, drinks, and fruits. Mama had a deep well in her compound, where she also raised fish. On one of our visits I remember relatives harvesting what looked like a massive catfish with a bucket, which was used to prepare *ofe nsala*, white soup. It was served with one of my favourite meals, pounded yam, which we cut and rolled into small balls that were dipped into the *ofe nsala* and swallowed whole.

The trips to Ikot Ekpene and Zaria raised a consciousness in me of my connection to a much larger cultural world, beyond Lagos and AN Barracks; a world shaped by my relatives who came in many appearances. They were uncles, aunts, in-laws, and cousins. They were tall, short, male, female, young, old, dark, light, small and heavy. They practised different faiths and spoke many languages. Memories of our distant trips outside Lagos were therefore important and we mostly preserved them with stories. But during one of our trips to Ikot Ekpene a photographer was invited to help capture and preserve the experience with images. I remember how he threw a piece of cloth over his head and the camera (which stood on a tripod) before taking pictures of us and our relatives, pictures that were all lost during the war.

Whether we visited Zaria or Ikot Ekpene, we were always

something of a curiosity and attracted long inquiring stares from relatives and indigenes alike, particularly in Ikot Ekpene. It may have had something to do with the fact that my father was an army officer, a rarity in those days, but I think some of it also had to do with my mother's mixed-race fair skin and dark curly hair.

Though we were content and had no reason to reside elsewhere, we eventually moved out of AN Barracks. When we did, it was as if we were going on a holiday trip. This was because we took with us what we usually took on vacations – clothing, towels, body lotions and combs. It therefore didn't strike me that our move was sudden and unusual and I didn't appreciate the urgency of the situation and the trauma that it must have caused my mother who had to organize us in the absence of my father. It wasn't until several months later and after more impromptu relocations and unexpected life changes that I realized that we hadn't really moved out of AN Barracks. We were forced out. After the second coup, our lives would have been in danger had we remained there. This explained why we hurriedly took just our basic needs with us, leaving behind our appliances, beds and other furniture. The second coup had been bloody and claimed many lives, one of which was supposed to be my father's. But he had escaped, at least temporarily, and his whereabouts were unknown. Even after the coup plotters successfully enthroned a new military government, neither they nor their supporters relented in their mission of hounding and killing mainly Igbo officers, though there were many non-Igbo targets too. One of them was my father whose *guilt* was by association with the former Igbo military head of state, General Aguiyi-Ironsi. His life was therefore still in danger, which meant that he could be in hiding for an unknown period. This was unnerving for my mother who was only thirty-one at the time.

We were forced out of AN Barracks forever and we left behind all that we had known and cherished. I missed the Army Children's School where I had been a pioneer student and where I had first learned to read and write. I was the only one in the family to attend that school. I missed our green uniforms laced with white designs, which were supposed to match the Nigerian flag. Because it was located in AN Barracks, it wasn't far from our house and I often walked there and back, usually in the company of my friend, Abasiefon, the son of Lieutenant Colonel Mfon George. Though Abasiefon and I lost contact after we left AN Barracks, we met again after the war when we both attended Holy Family College, a secondary school in Abak, a small town in the southeast of Nigeria. I missed the dedicated teachers, the afternoon snacks and the games we played. It was there that I first made personal friends, not family friends. I missed those friends, most of whom I would never see again.

We abandoned AN Barracks forever, failing to reap whatever we had sown there, and moved in with Mrs Faustina Adebisi Trimnell and her children who had found refuge on Spencer Street. Like my mother, Mrs Trimnell's husband, Lieutenant Colonel Rudolf Trimnell, was widely labelled *Ika-Igbo* or *midwestern Igbo*, and since anything Igbo was being hunted down like wild game by the second coup plotters, he was also in hiding. The large house on Spencer Street belonged to Mrs Trimnell's father and despite all that was done to make us feel at home, there were certain things I couldn't get used to, like collectively sleeping on mats in the living room, using bucket latrines and eating anywhere other than at a dining table. Though the home had been built for an extended family, it wasn't equipped to contain the crowd that suddenly descended on it. Besides Mrs Trimnell's father, a number of relatives resided there before she arrived with her children and their cousin, Celestine. And then we joined them, my mother with six children. Francis, now the youngest, was only a year old.

Organizing meals was quite a feat and despite the crowd we had breakfast, lunch and dinner each day. They were prepared in huge cauldrons that steamed over raw firewood flames on the veranda behind the home. Here, the women cut, ground, pounded, fried, boiled and stirred the meals. After we were done eating, they washed and scrubbed the pots, pans and dishes, and cleaned out the entire veranda, only to start the entire process again shortly thereafter. Gusts of thick sooty smoke eventually stained the ceiling, turning it black.

Once the meals were ready and announced, we – the Effiong and Trimnell children – lined up as in a boot camp and were served according to age. The routine soon became well defined and accepted. I was always served second-to-last, just before Titi. My mother, Mrs Trimnell, her father and other older adults were served separately and enjoyed privileges like chairs and table space. Toddlers like Francis were fed by their parents, servants or grown relatives.

I had always eaten at a dining table. Now, I settled for a spot on the bare floor, especially since I was at the bottom of the food chain. I had to give up on dessert, which had usually come in the form of an orange, a banana or, in rare cases, ice cream. I also had to give up on being served by a civilian or military servant. Reluctantly, I accepted reorientation at Spencer Street, but kept hoping for a return to AN Barracks.

Like cooking and feeding, bathing and sleeping arrangements had to be creative. Except for the adults and teenage children, we were bathed at the back of the house by our mothers, older relatives or servants. My mother would fill a plastic or metal bucket with heated water, sit on a low stool, and bathe us with a piece of soap and fibre sponge. Whenever it rained, we had to wait until the rain stopped before we took our baths. If it didn't stop, we went without bathing. I missed soaking in a bathtub.

At night, we, the children, both old and young, all slept on raffia mats spread out on the living room floor. This was after the chairs, side tables and other furniture were shifted to corners of the room. Because there weren't enough pillows to go around, most of us slept on the mats without them. The room was hot, and because the mosquitoes were plentiful, we spent a great part of the night swiping at them as they sang in our ears. The wrappers we covered ourselves with helped to protect us against the pests, but they did little against the heat.

In our discomfort we didn't only lose patience. We gradually learned how to survive. This became a cushion, the ability to carve out something that shielded us from the carnage that was slowing enveloping us. Before we dozed off individually on our mats, we poked fun at each other, cracked wild jokes and recalled what we thought were spectacular events of the day, colourless as they may have been. Despite the mosquitoes and heat, therefore, we embraced a world of exciting fantasy before we succumbed to sleep.

At Spencer Street I was introduced to another Lagos, one that we had been separated and shielded from by the safety and relative calmness of AN Barracks.

Though I had occasionally seen beggars on Lagos roads from the comfort of a car, for the first time I was seeing them up-close and in large numbers. They walked past the Trimnell home from the early hours of the morning until it got dark, soliciting for alms with chants that I didn't understand because they were delivered in unknown languages. They were almost always accompanied by helpers, usually children, perhaps their own, who supported and steered them in the right direction depending on the physical or mental ailment that was responsible for their destitution. It was anything from lost limbs to leprosy, from blindness to the dreaded elephantiasis that transformed a decent leg to a hideous mass of lumpy folding flesh.

The other Lagos did not only exist on the streets. It sometimes resided in the Trimnell home. Behind the main house, a path ran between the veranda-cum-kitchen and a wall that marked off another compound. A gate, which was shut at night, opened up onto this path, which served as another entry to the veranda and rooms at the rear of the home, including, regrettably, the building that housed the bucket toilets. If I had ever heard about bucket toilets, perhaps it was in light-hearted talk that hinted at a world much secluded from ours. The unsightly latrines, about three or four of them, were located somewhere behind the main building in a separate and smaller building that held adjoining booths. Using them became one of the most tedious and unpleasant challenges for me. While the stench was bad enough, an enthusiastic user occasionally aimed poorly and left tell-tale signs on the floor and squatting area. Fortunately, urinating, at least for the boys and men, was less taxing as it could be performed virtually anywhere outdoors.

One day, I had finished my business in the latrine and was about to step out. I put on my shorts, stepped down from the raised squatting section, opened the door and came face to face with a goat. My heart lost a few beats and throughout our chance meeting we stared at each other. I didn't budge and it didn't budge. For a while, neither one of us uttered a sound, not until I built the courage to begin to scream for help. I yelled and yelled and yelled until a boy, one of Mrs Trimnell's relatives, came to my rescue. He couldn't have been much older than me and hardly said anything. He simply grabbed the animal by its horns and pulled it away.

About once a week, the 'shit-carrier' arrived to empty the latrine buckets. He always had a filthy rag wrapped around his face. They say it wasn't just to protect himself against the smell; it was also in a bid to conceal his identity. He mounted a huge metal drum on his head into which he emptied the contents of the buckets. We always taunted him with songs and words that were uninspiring but made sure that we kept our distance when we did so. He was known to hurl his burden at his adversaries. When we weren't within firing range, he would go on to plaster portions of the compound. His main area of attack was the backyard as it served as an entry and exit point for him. Here, on certain days, he splattered chunks of excrement on the ground and dividing wall. But cooking had to go on, even if the audience sometimes comprised a cluster of excited flies.

Communal living at Spencer Street made it impossible to

keep personal secrets. It soon became public knowledge that I frequently wet the bed. At AN Barracks, I was periodically scoffed at for this weakness, but at least it was kept within the family. For entertainment, but usually when I got into an argument with anyone at Spencer Street, cheap shots were taken at me. The customary unrepentant mantra was, 'piss-piss for bed', which identified me as a habitual and repulsive bed wetter. Each assault hurt deeply and yet I had to amour myself and prepare for a lot more, for the condition wouldn't go away until I was sixteen.

Ibibio, our language, offered another cheap source of ridicule from other children in the compound. They would string meaningless sounds together in what was supposed to capture how crude and nonsensical Ibibio was. Since my parents were from different ethnic groups and spoke mostly English (despite my mother's growing mastery of Ibibio), we actually spoke more English than we did Ibibio in our home. But this didn't deter the children who were just doing what children do. In the end, their mockery was done in jest and not out of malice.

Whatever the ridicule, I remained a timid child that avoided any form of confrontation. I was therefore vulnerable and easy prey. When I was teased, I simply endured it as best as I could, in the hope that my tormentor would tire and leave me alone. It was therefore something of an anomaly when I decided to fight back one day. The fight didn't last long and I don't remember what it was about. In a matter of seconds, I was flat on my back and my head struck a stone, much to the delight of the crowd that had gathered to witness the spectacle. They cheered. I wailed for help and was relieved when Femi, the eldest of the Trimnell sons, came to my rescue. He pulled the lad off me and went on to serve him a slap or two. It was an unfair end to the scuffle, but I was delighted when the boy cried out in pain.

Things were no longer normal. But even when they were, back at AN Barracks, normalcy was occasionally threatened by a fistfight, sickness, or a disciplinary whack from my mother. Even when we visited the Trimnell home, we occasionally had to confront the unpredictable savagery of their pet monkey. We therefore learned the importance of pretence long before we were forced out of AN Barracks, especially when we were visited by a rare dark cloud.

At Spencer Street, when the dark cloud visited more regularly and became much larger, the need to fabricate contentment became even more necessary. We clung to this masquerade; it became one of our greatest survival companions from when the war raged in the months to come until long after it was officially over.

We weren't the only ones who manufactured laughter when there was no reason to laugh. So did the Trimnells who flirted with laughter, even revelry, in the most delightful way. One of the Trimnell daughters had a daughter of her own. We were still at Spencer Street when this beautiful girl turned one. An elaborate birthday party was thrown and many children, like me, were in attendance, dressed in our most colourful outfits. To the outsider it may not have looked like a children's party since there were perhaps more adults on hand to eat, drink and dance to highlife and juju music. I recall that the most popular dance of the day was *kpangolo*. Having just learned about the dance whose sprightly moves I tried unsuccessfully to accomplish, I preferred to just watch the experts do their thing.

In the end it wasn't *kpangolo* or the jollof rice and soft drinks that were the highlight for me; it was the plentiful pieces of sugarcane stalks. I had eaten sugarcane before but never seen it in such abundance. I chewed and sucked the sweet sap out of several small stems, though the process was tedious. This was because I first had to perform the difficult task of tearing off the tough skin with my teeth before getting to the white and easier-to-chew softer flesh in which the sweet sap was stored. It was almost ominous, this effort at finding sweetness within a shell that dissuaded me.

With all that was happening at Spencer Street, we were learning a vital lesson, though it was not apparent at the time. Choice was sometimes a luxury, not a right. Our circumstance was such that we were presented with very limited choices. The result was that we all had to readapt to a lifestyle that came with new and strict rules that I detested. I had never lived under conditions that were so stern and rigid in their expectations, or so regimented in their methods of executing law and order. I had been spoiled and was used to a daily sequence that had been orderly and firm, yet flexible and friendly. Now, I had to face another world that easily lost its patience and respected no sacred cows, not even if they had been birthed by lieutenant colonels.

But what tormented me most at Spencer Street was not the readjustments that had to be made. It was when my mother wept because my father's whereabouts were still unknown. Whenever she wept, I was at a loss and stared at her in silence as Mrs Trimnell tried to console her. She was sure that my father had been murdered. She was almost right.

The Spencer Street episode ended as dramatically as it had begun, putting a halt to all anxieties and speculations about my father. On the day of our departure, my brothers, sisters and my mother, were sneaked out of the compound under the cover of dark and delivered to a seaport. All I remember is that a car was on hand to receive us and was driven by an unknown man. The details are vague but later I learned that my father orchestrated everything. How he managed to do so from wherever he was hiding remains a mystery. We left our Spencer Street refuge and it was not until twenty-one or twenty-two years later that I again met Tony, Femi and Titi Trimnell at De Moines, Iowa, in the United States, having already met their sister, Rosemary, who briefly attended the same secondary school with me and my brothers in the 1970s.

Without the Trimnells, I cannot say what would have been our fate in Lagos at that time. Life was no longer sacred depending on whose it was, and that included ours. Without the Trimnells, we would have been vulnerable to so many things, and death may not have been the worst of those vulnerabilities. We will therefore be eternally grateful to the Trimnells.

Chapter 2

View from the mountain and the valley

At the seaport, I gazed at a ship that took on the form of a splendid mountain. We were soon guided into it. When the vessel began to move, we waved at a man who I initially thought was the one that had chauffeured us there. Then I noticed that the man stood beside a tiny two-door red car that I immediately recognized as my mother's Mini Moke. This confused me since it was not in this car that we had been transported to the seaport. I had not seen the Mini Moke since we left AN Barracks and would not see it again once the ship departed. My guess is that the strange man was the same man that had been teaching my mother how to drive, though from where he stood I couldn't make out his face. My mother had been learning to drive with this car and had made considerable progress before we had to leave AN Barracks, after which she put her driving lessons on hold. This was around late 1966 or early 1967. She would eventually resume her lessons and receive her license in Port Harcourt in 1983.

The ship was neat and stylish, and I recall a cosy compartment with bright colours in which every necessary thing was available. A world away from Spencer Street, it was like a benevolent giant that hovered above without dwarfing those it came in contact with, an ogre whose ferocity was shrouded in an inexplicable calm. My brothers and I spent a lot of time peering out of one of the portholes. Everything was blue – the massive waters below and the vast sky above, except at the point they met, which was anything from grey to orange depending on the time of day.

There was a white man who occasionally showed up. Sometimes his wife and son showed their faces too. They were courteous and friendly, especially the man, who smiled a lot. Later, I learned that he was the ship's captain. Otherwise, most of what happened on that trip remains hazy. I am not sure how long it lasted, perhaps a week or so, and then we finally arrived at Port Harcourt. My father was at the seaport to receive us in his usual manner, with warm hugs and smiles. We were relieved to see him after several weeks, especially with rumours that he was probably dead. My mother's excitement was beyond words.

My father had been in hiding in Lagos most of the time we had spent at Spencer Street. He eventually sneaked out and made his way to the east ahead of us and under circumstances that remained a mystery to me until after the war. But first, he had to escape from Kaduna where he had been Acting Commander of the First Brigade. He couldn't have accomplished this without help from Major Samuel Ogbemudia, his Brigade Major; Reverend John McCarthy, the Kaduna Archbishop; the American Embassy in Kaduna and a host of other friends and acquaintances. Disguised in a *babariga* (a typical Hausa outfit), a fez and dark glasses, he made his final exit from Kaduna on a train ride that took him to Lagos. In Lagos, friends like Mr George Sheen, Mr M. A. Arogundade and Mr Victor Vonnick were on hand to guarantee his safety and anonymity, at great risk. My father continued to move from place to place until Mr Vonnick was able to provide the funds that were used to hire a taxi that took him to Enugu in the east. The kind Mr Vonnick accompanied him on the long trip. Fortunately, he was not recognized or apprehended throughout.

We soon loaded our few belongings into a car and, as we drove off, the magic of the huge vessel and the enigma of its captain, his wife and son, gradually vanished in the background and became concealed by events that didn't lie too far ahead. Our destination was Ikot Ekpene.

Ikot Ekpene, a small rural, but commercially active, town was the antithesis of Lagos. It was serene though it boasted a vibrant communal culture of constant and informal interaction between the people, during which they shared meals, exchanged stories and sheltered one another. Like most residents, we had a family compound and moved in there after we arrived from Port Harcourt. Our family compound can be understood in terms of a piece of land on which a main house stands with separate outbuildings to the rear occupied by family members. We stayed in the main house, part of which was already occupied by my father's older brother, Etok á Papa, his wife, two sons and two daughters. Though we were from Ibiono, Ikot Ekpene was our adopted home. My father's father, whom we called Ekamba Ete, Grandfather, chose Ikot Ekpene for refuge around 1929 and relocated his family from Aba, a commercial Igbo city and my father's birthplace. It all happened after the historic Eastern Women's Revolution of the same year, in which my grandmother had participated. For fear of retribution against his wife by the colonial government, Grandfather left Aba with her and their two sons, my father being the younger. Ikot Ekpene was a good choice because it was not too far from Ibiono and boasted a commercial promise that Grandfather didn't want to completely abandon. In time, he became a renowned local doctor, purchased a piece of land and erected a two-room mud building on what would eventually be known as 55 Umuahia Road. This building doubled as his personal residence and hospital-shrine. It had a bedroom and another room, a dark one, that was full of mystique and served as a consultation and healing room. Here, he received and treated patients with ailments that ranged from the natural to the spiritual. As he married more wives, Grandfather built more mud homes to accommodate them and their children.

My father would later erect a cement home on his father's land; it was one of the first in Ikot Ekpene and stood in front of the compound, soon taking on the status of 'main building'. Not long before the tragic incidents of 1966, my father paid for the construction of another building behind the main one. It contained my mother's kitchen, a dining area, a shower room and a toilet.

But we didn't spend much time in Ikot Ekpene; it was a temporary layover before we proceeded to Enugu, which was then the capital of the Eastern Region and home to the Governor, Lieutenant Colonel Chukwuemeka Odumegwu-Ojukwu. I liked the hilly, stony, red dusty landscape in which Enugu was wrapped. It was a beautiful, neat and peaceful city with a striking road network that maintained a calmness despite its busyness. Enugu was not Lagos nor Ikot Ekpene. It was alive without being noisy, grand but not intimidating. It was alluring and modern without being too mechanical; it was fragrant and simple without being rural.

We spent about two weeks with the family of one Mr Ibok in Enugu's expansive Government Reserved Area, GRA, an indication that our move to Enugu was hurried. GRA originally provided housing for colonial officials in a designated suburban location and was called the 'European Quarters'. After Nigeria gained independence, homes in the area were reallocated to top civil servants who essentially replaced the Europeans.

Things were uneventful and typical family life went on without a hitch, though we were slightly cramped in Mr Ibok's small flat. But its modern amenities made things bearable. We moved out of Mr Ibok's flat after my father was assigned a house at 4 Manua Street, also in the GRA. Overlooking a major highway, it was a modest bungalow of about three bedrooms; we were happy with the basic comfort it provided. This was the first time since AN Barracks that we were again living independently without feeling like we were a nuisance. We were free to prosper or make mistakes without scrutiny from anyone.

It had been several months since we enjoyed the luxury of watching television, which soon became a key part of our evening rituals. Much like the television we had owned at AN Barracks, this one was small and black, transmitted in black-and-white and provided the thrill that we needed. Local shows came in the form of dramas, dance band entertainments and variety shows like *Ukonu's Club*. We also cherished the foreign shows that typically crowned television broadcasts each day, including *The Beverly Hillbillies*, *I Love Lucy*, Bugs Bunny cartoons and films featuring cowboys and Indians, Tarzan the ape-man and superheroes like John Wayne.

To help with domestic work, a young man, Victor, arrived from Ikot Ekpene and served faithfully until the end of the impending war. He remained a close friend of the family after the war at which time he was hired as a lorry driver for my father's business before setting up his own business. My father's younger brother, Etim, also moved in with us and helped with various chores. His presence came as no surprise since he had been a frequent visitor to AN Barracks and, in his usual way, was charming, told us stories and gave us lessons in Ibibio. But at this time Etim wanted to do more than help around the house and informed my father that he wanted to join the army. I am not sure whether he said it seriously or in jest, but my father went ahead and helped him enlist. At one point, he became my father's batman and before the war ended attained the modest rank of sergeant.

4 Manua was surrounded by a large field that flaunted shrubs and mango trees. My brothers and I played and ran around the compound, sometimes taking breaks to observe the traffic that flowed below. For the most part, life was uncomplicated and uneventful.

My older brothers, Valentine and Charles, attended All Saints Primary School in the GRA while I was sent to Sancta Maria in Uwani, one of Enugu's business districts. I imagine this was because All Saints didn't have a nursery school, which I hadn't yet completed. Rosalyn and Mercy were sent to Cornelia Cornelly College, a secondary school in Uyo, which is about seventeen miles from Ikot Ekpene.

Sancta Maria had a compound that was vast and neat. Its rich green fields may have clashed with our white upon blue uniforms, but it couldn't have been too harsh on the naked eye. After my first day at school I was sent home to take tutorials that prepared me for admission into Elementary One. My mother's teacher-training background came in very handy and she taught me, mostly with *udara* seeds, which she used for lessons in addition and subtraction. After the orange, sweet (although sometimes sour) fruit was eaten, its large, canoe-shaped black seeds were sucked clean and preserved in cans or other containers where they dried out. Except for when we used them as missiles in mock battles; the dried seeds were very useful as an arithmetic aid. My mother also coached me in reading and writing. In the end, I was mentally prepared to attend Sancta Maria.

The school was decent and full of activity. Besides quality lessons, during break periods the boys played football, ran around noisily and sometimes broke into fistfights. The girls formed separate cliques and played what we described as girls' games. I was usually content to just watch and take in everything from a distance. My only dilemma came in the form of a classmate, a girl. We shared a low table around which about four chairs were arranged. Periodically, she would kick me under the table, at which I would give her a look that questioned the unprovoked attack. Her usual response would be to kick me several more times. "Say me sorry!" She would demand with each kick. Her impunity added insult and venom to injury. If I didn't give in to her demand, she kicked me some more. I always conceded and said "sorry", before bowing my head in humiliation.

I still attended Sancta Maria when we moved from Manua Street to 6 Park Lane, also in the GRA. A large lorry made a few trips between the locations as it conveyed our property to our new home. Each time it paused at 4 Manua, we, the boys, climbed into the back of the lorry where we played a series of invented games until the military and civilian workers began to load things into the back of the vehicle. We only added nuisance value to their labours.

6 Park Lane was also a modest bungalow with two or three bedrooms. I later gathered that my mother had hated 4 Manua because of its unique architecture. To use the restroom, one

had to step outdoors and walk through the front veranda. During the day this wasn't much of a problem, but at night it caused enough concern. Otherwise, 6 Park Lane had no real advantage; in fact, it might actually have been slightly smaller. My father had apparently refused the large two-story homes that were allocated to senior officers. But the decision to accept a smaller home turned out to be an error we would later pay dearly for.

Though much of the comfort and contentment of AN Barracks had been salvaged, it did not last. When the disruption came, it left an indelible mark. In truth, there had never been total calm. Just as it had been when things were first disrupted in Lagos, I felt an enduring air of anxiety; I knew something was brewing and would soon boil over.

When the calm was first interrupted, it came in the form of parades that were led mostly by young men, but young women also participated and so did the middle-aged. From a young age, I was familiar with, and fascinated by, military parades. But these parades were different and were not led by military personnel. They were performed on the streets and had no particular order to them except for a voice that was raised high above the rest and led the marchers in a defiant chant.

Why do you delay? Come and save your nation,
Why do you delay? Come and save your nation,
Why do you delay? Come and save your nation,
O Biafrans, why do you delay?

We are Biafrans fighting for survival
In the name of Jesus, we shall conquer

The participants carried sticks and any other object that signified weaponry and a willingness to do battle. Even though I had witnessed parades where real rifles were carried, I had not felt threatened by them because they were always wielded with discipline and precision. Essentially, I perceived them more as theatrical props than weapons. But these street parades, because they were rowdy in a free-spirited sort of way, they transformed sticks and branches into weapons of terror. From our compound at 4 Manua and later at 6 Park Lane, we witnessed the processions as they snaked by until the chants, songs and marchers faded in the distance. Without specific knowledge of their mission or destination, it was clear, however, that they prepared for a bitter confrontation somewhere in the near future, one that would turn out to be senseless, rotten and fierce.

There were other unsavoury hints of conflict, like the day at school when an alarm disrupted our usual schedule, followed by frantic directives by our teachers that we all step outside. Here, we were forced to lie flat on the green fields. I periodically raised my head and looked around, catching glimpses of the blue and white uniforms that dotted the compound. We spent about thirty minutes in that position and would learn that it was an air raid drill. Of course, the reference to air raid did not have the impact it should have had on me, not yet. When some of us inquired out of curiosity, school officials were not necessarily euphemistic in telling us that it was a very dangerous situation where enemy planes dropped bombs that destroyed buildings and killed people. If that were the case, I wondered how lying in an open field would provide protection. Still, it was only reality that could relay the severity of what was anticipated and, until the planes actually zoomed in and dropped bombs, I saw no reason to panic.

The gathering storm, a phenomenon that still seemed relatively removed from our life, came closer to us with the arrival of the destitute woman and her children. I think the oldest was a boy, and together with relatives and the house help, they numbered about seven. Although their story initially lacked details, it was part of a familiar theme of death and destruction at the time. They had escaped the massacre of easterners in Abeokuta, even though the woman's husband had been killed. When they descended on us, 6 Park Lane proved to be too small for the crowd. At the time, my father and mother probably regretted not taking one of the larger homes that senior officers were entitled to. But they welcomed the woman and her entourage with open arms and, for a while, the atmosphere of Spencer Street returned. The main difference was that this was our home.

I didn't lose my sleeping space, which means that alternative sleeping arrangements were made for the woman and her children. But we all ate at the same dining table around which, somehow, enough chairs were arranged to accommodate the crowd.

Notwithstanding the anxiety that came with marchers stoking war and frightening stories told by the destitute woman, we didn't think there was much to worry about. We even found time to embark on a trip, though it was just Charles and I that were sent to Amawbia, a village in Awka, to spend a few days with my mother's older sister, Mama Nkechi, who doted on us with a fervour that we were not used to. Mama Nkechi translates literally to Nkechi's Mother. In Nigeria, the reference to a parent as mother or father of a particular child is prevalent. Several reasons account for the use of a specific child's name in this way. He or she could be an only child, a first child, a last child, an only male or female child, a first male or female child, or a child thought to be favoured by a parent or both parents. In this instance, Nkechi was her parents' first daughter. We ate, rested and played to our hearts' content. Whenever we were asked what we wanted to eat, Charles asked for plantains while I requested rice, and despite the extra effort it took, the separate meals were prepared each time. It was a visit filled with much warmth and, for the first and only time, I ate starch, which was bright yellow because Mama Nkechi had coloured it with palm oil. Though it was a meal she had prepared for herself, when Charles and I asked what it was out of curiosity, she informed us with a measure of amused revelation and went on to ask us if we wanted to taste it. It was all the motivation we needed. We ate with our fingers by 'cutting' and rolling the gooey meal into small balls, which we dipped in a vegetable sauce before swallowing them whole. Mama Nkechi was the classic sweet aunt with whom we could get away with things that our parents would absolutely not tolerate. We took advantage and were not bashful about asking for sweets and choice foods. After spending about two weeks in Amawbia, we returned to Enugu.

One day, as dramatically as the destitute woman and her children had appeared, they disappeared. I remember not seeing them and not bothering about when or how they had left, or where they had gone. They simply faded away and little or nothing was said about them. Later I learned that the woman was the wife of Lieutenant Gabriel Okonweze, former commander of the Abeokuta Garrison. He had been murdered during the second coup, his crime being that he was from Asaba, a major Igbo city in modern-day Delta State.

Chapter 3

The rising sun that kept rising

The sudden appearance and disappearance of Mrs Okonweze didn't remotely compare with the threat of war that was steadily descending on us, even if occasional distractions painted a different picture. Like the day my father returned from work and everyone said congratulations to him. I also congratulated him though I didn't know why. I asked and was told that he had been promoted to the rank of a one-star general, a brigadier. Soon, therefore, he was entitled to an entourage of about two or three vehicles that accompanied him to and from work, loaded with armed soldiers. The euphoria changed, however, when the guns were turned on us.

The first time was early one morning when we were rudely awakened by a house help and the sound of gunfire. Because there was a sense of urgency in his voice, we dashed outside in our sleeping clothes to observe my father wielding a machine gun, though he still wore the wrapper and vest he had gone to bed in. There was pandemonium as people screamed and hurried to nowhere in particular. High in the sky, a jet whooshed back and forth. It was uncanny as I was used to aircraft flying by and disappearing in the distance. But this one seemed to be undecided and kept going and coming. Each time the plane was in sight, my father took aim and fired at it with his machine gun. As instructed, we took cover behind the house until the plane eventually disappeared. My father's military aides then set out to gather the empty shells that his rifle had coughed up.

Sadly, much worse was to come, and sooner than I anticipated.

It happened early that evening as my two older brothers and I played behind the house. When we first heard the booming sounds, we suspected thunder. But they continued and were marked by piercing howls that increased as they got closer. By the time we realized that it wasn't thunder, all of Enugu seemed to have come to the same realization. The streets were soon filled with people in disarray, fleeing to everywhere at once and screaming in panic. Because our gardener lay on the ground and covered his head with dry leaves and branches, we did the same. Our cook, whom we called Akataka, suddenly dashed out in full army gear, carrying a rifle and wearing a helmet covered with leaves. I'm not sure what he hoped to achieve when he got to the road and started to scream wildly at people and vehicles that sped by.

Enugu was being shelled and, to this day, I shudder at the memory of those terrifying blasts. The city was about to fall into the hands of an enemy that had finally opted for violence over diplomacy. Before long, that enemy was cited as Nigeria and its leader was Lieutenant Colonel Yakubu Gowon; they steadily became synonymous with everything repulsive and depraved. We had to disconnect from them, and we did so by way of a nobler and more compassionate creation, Biafra, whose leader, Ojukwu, was dominating a lot of news and gossip. He was the messiah that would enable the rebirth that Biafra promised. Thereafter, it was drilled into us through propaganda and songs that our identity had been renewed forever because we now belonged to Biafra. Central to our rebirth were a flag, proudly flaunting a rising sun, and an anthem that proclaimed our sovereignty and dignity.

On the same day that Enugu was shelled, we fled the city,

abandoning most of our property. Our destination was Ikot Ekpene, and although my father arranged our departure, he didn't come with us. Mama Nkechi, my mother's older sister who was visiting at the time, accompanied us with her youngest child, Chidozie. It was almost dark when we arrived at Ikot Ekpene. A few days later, Mama Nkechi's other children joined us from Amawbia – Victor, Nkechi, Sonny and Nneka – accompanied by two young servants, a boy, Simon, who had to be eight or nine, and an equally young girl.

The war had begun in earnest and for the next two-and-a-half years I would be a dedicated and firm believer in the magnificent Biafran dream.

Ikot Ekpene was the archetypal large village with hints of urban life. Aside from its growing business activities, bicycles were still its main means of commercial transport. The transporters, simply referred to as cyclists, could be recognized by the black face-caps they wore. When you required the services of one, all you did was yell out, "Cyclist!" as they rode by. Young people like me were typically made to sit on the front crossbar, especially if a parent were there to straddle the back carriage. Otherwise, the back carriage was the standard passenger seat when luggage wasn't mounted on it.

Because my father set up his headquarters at the Central Bible Institute, CBI, in Umuahia shortly after Enugu's collapse, he didn't spend much time in Ikot Ekpene. He occasionally appeared with his military entourage and, in a day or two, would disappear. CBI was among several academic institutions that were converted to garrisons, refugee camps, or health centres during the war. My father's residence stood at the highest point of the campus; this is where the European principal of the Institute once stayed. Behind it was a huge valley, one of Umuahia's natural attractions. Because Umuahia was a relatively short distance from Ikot Ekpene, about a thirty-minute drive, we visited my father quite frequently.

At Ikot Ekpene, we could pretend that all was well, thanks largely to Grandfather. Taller than any of his numerous children, Grandfather was a sight to behold and exuded confidence, dignity and serenity. He walked tall, literally, and from whatever angle one viewed things, he was hardly like his son, my father. Not in clothing, religion, food, leisure or lifestyle; they lived in different worlds. Whereas most of us worshipped at the Catholic Church with a degree of loyalty, he wasn't a Christian. This was not at all a source of friction. He was a renowned local doctor that relied on herbs, roots and spiritual guidance. One evening, he had me and my brothers drink a bitter fluid from a snail's shell. To this day I don't know what it was but believe it had lifelong therapeutic attributes as it came from a grandfather who loved his grandchildren deeply. In another instance, when my right arm swelled up, it was Grandfather who provided the first soothing antidote to my pain after he rubbed onto it a substance made from crushed leaves or roots.

But Grandfather's gift for healing wasn't always as plain as leaves and roots. My brothers and I visited his modest restaurant one afternoon and noticed with curiosity how a dead owl, *nkuriku,* dangled from a pole at the back of the building. Inquiry soon revealed that the owl was actually a witch that had been apprehended and killed in a battle that Grandfather waged in the supernatural world. What we were seeing was the body that the witch had inhabited to carry out its night flights and torment its victims. But to fully kill the witch, the bird had to be boiled in a special pot drilled with holes at the base. A date was set on which my brothers and I, Grandfather and one of our young uncles, Edet, gathered at a place in the bush that bordered the house to carry out the ritual. We all sat on low stools in a circle as the owl was then boiled. Much to my amazement, water did not leak through the holes at the bottom of the pot. But even more astonishing was what happened when a light rain began to fall. Edet cut down a few palm branches and thrust them in the ground, arranging them in a circle around us. The rain continued to fall, but not a drop fell within the circle that Edet had created; we stayed dry. If my innocent eyes were deceiving me, then Grandfather must have drugged us to achieve this deception.

In the mornings, we assembled on the veranda of Grandfather's shrine-cum-home where he lit a fire with pieces of wood. The flames warmed us and were also used to heat up bathing water or prepare boiled plantains in a zesty broth. At other times, Grandfather ordered the slaughter of a goat or chickens, and the meat was either used to prepare pepper-soup or was roasted over raw flames and thoroughly spiced. Sometimes I got to sip a little palm-wine at these festive occasions, but under no circumstance was I allowed to touch *kai-kai*, the concentrated and acerbic gin that was fermented from palm-wine, and which frequently found its way to Grandfather's gatherings. The ensuing feast was usually concluded when Grandfather hammered out a tune on his drum and sang a few songs; we sang and danced along.

Ikot Ekpene was never boring and, besides Grandfather's celebrations, excitement showed up in other ways. At night, children from our compound and neighbouring compounds played games, particularly hide and seek. The games were so electrifying they sometimes went on to as late as midnight. We retired to our various homes and beds, dusty and sweaty.

When the thatched roofs were leaking and needed patching or replacing, we had fun using thin, sliced palm bamboo sticks to weave together *nkanya*, the frond mats that were used to build new roofs.

The masquerade season came and we anticipated with enthusiasm, and some unease, the arrival of the *Ekpo*, spirit masquerades that were dark black because they painted their entire bodies with charcoal mixed with palm oil. Their masks ranged from ordinary to ferocious and were partially held down by layers of raffia and various types of leaves. Their waists and groin area were covered by short raffia skirts or strips of cloth; their buttocks were usually bare. Dangling from their waists were scabbards that housed machetes, though their preferred weapons were the bows and arrows for which they were notorious. There were horrid tales of violence that cited vicious use of the machetes and bows and arrows.

Once the *Ekpo* masquerades showed up, we retreated to watch from the safety of our veranda. When they ventured into our compound, we disappeared into the house and peeped through windows. It was especially an abomination for girls and women to hang around when the masquerades were in the vicinity. The lesser *Ekpo Ntogoyen*, youthful spirits, emerged around the same time. More of a sideshow than the main act of the *Ekpo* masquerades, these ones comprised male adolescents that coated themselves in *ndom*, a white chalky substance. Although they didn't instil much fear, we were slightly apprehensive of them because they also wielded bows and arrows.

The masquerades were members of a larger male-only *Ekpo*

Society, which has existed for centuries and predated colonial intrusion. They originally played political roles as community decision-makers and also served as embodiments of the spirits of their ancestors. The latter status afforded them the power to provide divine protection and guidance to their communities.

Funerals added their own brand of entertainment and charged atmosphere to Ikot Ekpene. They were a time of liberal eating, drinking and celebration; a time when limits were not placed on who was welcome or unwelcome at a homestead. The amount you ate and drank depended on the wealth of the hosts and your capacity to hold your food and drink. Burial processions quite often danced past our home because Umuahia Road was one of Ikot Ekpene's main thoroughfares. The pageantry was always colourful, partly because people wore their best outfits, but also because of the ruckus brought on by music and song. Amid everything, a degree of solemnity was preserved by the coffin that was usually hoisted on the heads or shoulders of male family members of the deceased. The sight was familiar, even expected, except for the day when the coffin didn't seem to cooperate with its carriers who were constantly tossed back and forth. The men had taken off their shirts because of the amount of energy they exerted in trying to restrain the stubborn casket. They sweated profusely. If they were acting, they were doing a marvellous job. At a point, the men began to spin around in circles in the middle of the road, still holding tight to the box and bringing traffic to a standstill. News soon spread that the deceased was bent on visiting a number of friends before being laid to rest. He thus took control of the pallbearers rather than vice versa. The story sparked off as much concern as it did hilarity, but all vestiges of the latter vanished when, on arriving at the front of our home, the coffin and its entourage veered sharply into our compound. Most of us fled indoors, not waiting to find out who the deceased had come to wish farewell to.

We returned to school, though it was just me and my two older brothers. At first, my mother had arranged for us to be tutored by two teachers in a private home where one or two rooms served as classrooms. Here we received basic information in a monotonous setting. It was about a mile from the house, which made it easy for Goddy, my mother's driver, to chauffeur us back and forth. Goddy's contract with my mother was unusual, since he owned the car with which he served her. We attended this 'school' for a few weeks and then transferred to the more conventional primary school at Ifuho, a section of Ikot Ekpene about two miles from our home. Though Goddy sometimes chauffeured us to this school too, at other times we walked. It was the longest walk I had undertaken at the time. Edet, our young uncle, attended with us. Though modest, the school was good. But Biafra didn't have the resources to fund its schools and this one was soon closed down.

At Ikot Ekpene, the spectacle, randomness and exciting anticipations of everyday life – Grandfather's celebrations, the appearance of masquerades, close-knit friendships, family bonding and temporary schooling – were so powerful that they built an imaginary wall that seemed to shield the small town from the rest of the country. It remained a fantasy haven until a man and woman arrived at our compound fleeing a threat that had forced them out of Oron, about sixty miles away. They warned us that the enemy had already overrun the ancient city of Calabar to the east, which, by ferry, is about an hour and a half from Oron. Although my father wasn't at home, their message was most likely for him, perhaps to alert him of the need to assemble a protective army against the advancing enemy. News from the man and woman, especially in my father's absence, reintroduced the type of anxiety that we had left behind in Enugu. They departed after delivering their message. Leaving us tense and unsettled.

But it wasn't only strangers from faraway places that reminded us of the encroaching danger. One afternoon, an open truck carrying a few Biafran soldiers stopped in front of our neighbour's house. Because the truck periodically drove down Umuahia Road and past our house, at first it attracted little attention. But things changed when the Biafran soldiers marched into the house, emerging several minutes later with the patriarch of the family, Mr Okon Patrick, whose two sons, Eno and Reuben, were our friends. A crowd slowly gathered as he was led to the truck and ushered into one of the back seats. Mr Patrick looked distraught and terrified. After the Biafran soldiers got back into the truck, they drove off and the crowd dispersed.

Mr Patrick never returned to his house. After the war, I heard different versions of how he had died, with all versions admitting that Biafran soldiers were responsible. One common rumour accused him of being a traitor who publicly maligned the Biafran cause, for which my father allegedly cautioned him to be less outspoken because of the likelihood of state retaliation. There may be some truth to the latter since many non-Igbo easterners were distrusting and critical of Biafra. Failing to heed my father's warning, Mr Patrick's arrest was ordered by Mr Akpan Ekukinam-Bassey, the Administrator of the Annang Province, under which Ikot Ekpene was a district. However, it was my father that was blamed for Mr Patrick's arrest and eventual death, a charge circulated by his family and the Ikot Ekpene community. My father, on the other hand, didn't want to come across as favouring a neighbour or overstepping his authority, especially since there were other detainees on whose behalf he had not interceded. He therefore left the matter to Ekukinam-Bassey who refused to release Mr Patrick, not even after my mother intervened. As the war progressed and detainees were constantly relocated under increasingly desperate conditions, Mr Patrick's whereabouts became unknown. He apparently died in detention.

Whatever the truth, the incident has left me confused and uncomfortable. Mr Patrick simply didn't deserve to die. The assassination of non-Igbos by Biafran soldiers has provoked much controversy and deep feelings of resentment against Igbos by non-Igbos, which still persists. It is another sad aspect of the war and a reminder of how erstwhile friendly neighbours became enemies and turned on one another with unthinkable hostility.

After the war, some of my non-Igbo friends told stories of how members of their families had been murdered by Igbo Biafrans, both soldiers and civilians. One was a girlfriend who I had met at the University of Calabar where we were both students. Whenever I visited her family; her brother, sisters and mother treated me with utmost respect and kindness. If they held any animosity against my father for being a top officer in the army that was liable for the death of their father and husband, they didn't show it. The same was true of Mr Patrick's family, even if they may have carried suppressed feelings of bitterness. After the war, we re-established the pre-war friendship that we had maintained for many years. I am content with not being confronted by these families over my father's role during the war. I have also carefully avoided broaching the subject with them.

The thought of Mr. Patrick or anyone in Ikot Ekpene being anti-Biafra was confusing and difficult to swallow. After all, Ikot Ekpene had a dominant Biafran presence that was evident in the Biafran army units that dotted sections of the town. Biafran soldiers were a common sight and they seemed to be widely accepted and respected with no hints of resentment against them. Each day, radio announcements condemned Gowon and urged gallant Biafrans to take up arms and protect their precious land from his invading Nigerian army. We were warned of their devious determination to take control of our rich oil fields and were reminded of their recent genocidal attacks on our people in the north, which is precisely why Biafra, as one song stated, was 'our land of freedom'.

But bravado and virtue could not prevent the greater threat that was approaching. When it arrived, it completely took Ikot Ekpene off-guard and brought the war to our doorstep. It happened one evening when, strangely, two planes flew side by side above the town. They almost faded in the distance but turned around and headed back, after which one of them nosedived and released a black object that landed some distance away, producing a loud explosion. Later we learned that the bomb had hit our former school at Ifuho. Ikot Ekpene came alive and hysterical crowds flooded its streets in every direction. The culprit was described as a vicious attacker from the north and, from all that was told, I fabricated a terrifying monster that was large, dark, covered in tribal scars, exceptionally hideous and blatantly ruthless.

Shortly after, rumours foretold plane loads of enemy soldiers parachuting into Ikot Ekpene, for which young men were immediately mobilized to cut long branches that were fashioned into pointed, javelin-style poles. These were then planted in open fields with their sharp tips facing skywards, ensuring that the enemy would meet a very painful landing if indeed he dared attempt an aerial invasion. When the enemy showed up months later, he didn't fall from the sky as many had predicted; he came by road. But I don't know whether his decision had anything to do with the shafts planted in the fields.

War had finally come to Ikot Ekpene.

We continued to go on occasional trips to Umuahia to spend time with my father who had recently been promoted to major general. But the enemy's threat to Ikot Ekpene drew ever closer, forcing us to relocate permanently to Umuahia. Mama Nkechi also moved to Umuahia with her five children and resided close to us. We visited each other quite frequently.

Embellished with valleys, Umuahia was the opposite of Enugu and its hills, and its gravels, were nothing like the red gravels of Enugu. Even more unlike Enugu were Umuahia's brown, rust-red and black millipedes which could be found everywhere. Sometimes, when a door or window was left open, they crawled into our home. In time, we got used to the multi-legged creatures.

CBI, where my father had set up his headquarters, flaunted a landscape that was breathtaking. It was a huge piece of land practically surrounded by mango trees of every kind. At the entrance to the Institute was a sentry post that opened up to a long uphill road that had lost most of its tar, so that what was left, if anything, was negligible and overtaken by sand. It stretched past empty classrooms and student dormitories now occupied by soldiers directly under my father's command, while, at the top of the incline, our home stood adjacent to staff homes taken up by my father's senior aides. Our home was bounded to the rear by a massive valley that we sometimes ventured into: me, my brothers, children from the neighbourhood and our cousins, Victor and Sonny.

There was a lot of space for play and we played. We explored the compound around us and the grounds surrounding the classrooms, dormitories and staff homes. The mango trees were alluring and we invaded them, sometimes not giving the mangoes enough time to ripen before we plucked them. The cashew trees weren't as numerous, but they suffered the same fate. We played football with children who descended on the camp, attracted to its open fields. Sometimes we visited the soldiers in their dormitories where they thrilled us with battle stories and showed off their rifles. Otherwise, we imitated them when they marched or practiced various drills.

Our interest was immediately aroused after we discovered a store wedged between two classrooms. It must once have served as a mini convenience store for students and staff of the Institute and carried mostly stationery. But it also carried packets of cigarettes. We found a way to open the window and periodically looted it under the leadership of Victor, our big cousin. We rarely put what we stole to good use, usually damaging them at play, or simply losing them. Then we started to help ourselves to packets of cigarettes and, at first, gave them to our soldier friends who were delighted to accept the rare gift, unconcerned about where we had got them from. But we soon gave in to temptation, or curiosity, and began to smoke the cigarettes ourselves, making sure that we did everything humanly possible to hide the truth from my mother and father. But my mother was notorious for catching thieves and unearthing ungodly secrets. I don't know what she was looking for in a carpenter's shed near the house – one of our smoking hideouts – when she noticed some empty packets of cigarette on the floor and on the tables. To make things worse, partially and fully smoked stubs were scattered all over the floor. My mother immediately gathered a few empty packets and confronted me before anyone else. It was a good strategy; she knew that I was the most likely culprit to buckle under interrogation. She didn't have to place too much pressure on me either.

"Who has been smoking all these cigarettes?" she inquired. "If you tell me the truth, you won't be punished, I promise. I will even give you a prize."

I fell for the ploy and sang like a bird, going into sacred details. As immediate reward for my confession, I received a swift slap to the side of my head. I was then ordered to kneel on the concrete pavement in front of the house as my mother sent for my brothers. Victor, the head culprit, was conveniently back at his mother's home. Shortly after my brothers arrived and saw me kneeling; they didn't even bother to lie when they were questioned. They too were ordered to kneel on the concrete and we remained there for about two hours until my father returned from work. He received the traditional salute from his orderly and walked into the house as if we didn't exist. It was about another hour before he emerged again. He was tying a wrapper around his waist and had on a vest, which was his usual attire of relaxation when he returned from work. My mother must have informed him of our crime as he wasted no time in sending for a cane. Because I was the youngest, I received only three strokes. I'm not sure how many Charles received, but Valentine received the most, anything from fifteen to twenty-four lashes. We wailed. Cigarettes have not appealed to me since.

Private tutors were again hired to teach us; two classrooms served as a makeshift school that was also attended by children of the late Aguiyi-Ironsi. There was Louisa, Fortune, Jennifer, Ann, Angela and Big and Little John. Victor also attended. We were simply separated into two groups. The older children of both families, including Rosalyn, Mercy and Victor, occupied one class, while the younger children, including me, Valentine and Charles, occupied the other. Somehow, two teachers were able to map out a schedule where they taught us different things based on our individual academic skills and levels. In what should have been a chaotic situation, a degree of order was actually maintained. But when things heated up in Umuahia, the school died a natural and predictable death. A prophetic display of this demise took place when one of the teacher's normal routines was ruthlessly upset by news that her sister had been badly injured in an air attack. Shocked by the news, she went into a state of panic in front of the school building, shrieking, lamenting and calling out the name of her sister whose life was now in the balance. Her anguish came to a climax when she threw herself on the ground and began to roll and thrash about, still unleashing her requiem. She naturally had to cut short her workday and was eventually escorted out of the camp by friends and sympathizers. We never saw her again.

Chapter 4

Red skies, red rain

Unlike the suspense of Enugu and Ikot Ekpene, Umuahia left us in no doubt that a war raged unceremoniously and unpredictably around us. At first, when my brothers and I climbed down into and explored the deep valleys around us, we did so for the risky thrill, to satisfy our curiosities and to discover the unknown. Then we were drawn into the frenzy of searching the bushes for 'enemies', sometimes going out on our own, sometimes going in the company of friends we had made inside and outside the camp, and sometimes accompanying a group of soldiers. Even my father was the occasional leader on those reconnaissance trips through the bushes, which we simply referred to as 'recces'. We walked long distances through steep unfriendly terrain that was rocky and thorny. The valleys were not always deep, but they were there, and trekking into and out of them blocked any hopes of staving off fatigue. An armed soldier or two always came along, which was a source of comfort. One day, my father was saved by his boots when he stepped onto a serrated iron trap, which reminded us that wild animals were also there to worry about. And, who knows, perhaps the fear of lurking 'enemies' may not have been fantasy. Mercy, who suffered frequent dizzy spells, participated in some of the recces. She almost always suffered an attack and had to be hoisted on an adult's back the rest of the way.

Air raids intensified at Umuahia; they got so frequent that we got used to them, or at least desensitized to them. To protect ourselves, roofs and sometimes entire buildings were draped in palm fronds. Bunkers were built, even if they served a psychological role more than anything else, for they would sink without resistance if they were hit by bombs, burying their occupants. The concept was simple. A large trench was dug and tree trunks were laid across it. A rich mound of earth was then heaped on the trunks and sometimes camouflaged with palm fronds and branches. Next, two entrances were dug into both sides of the trench. During an air raid, we ran into and remained in the chamber until there was enough evidence that the bombers had left. Sometimes, we didn't have to spend too long in the bunkers; at other times, we did. At least on one occasion we spent the entire day in a bunker. It was Christmas Day and the enemy were relentless in their efforts to make sure that Biafra didn't celebrate. That day, chairs and stools were delivered to the vault and we were served and ate our meals there, briefly stepping out only when we had to relieve ourselves. Rosalyn devised a strategy that helped us make the best of the situation, leading us in Christmas carols throughout the time we were holed up. A regular companion in the bunkers were earthworms and, of course, millipedes. To this day, I can smell the inside of the bunkers and the rich dark soil they were dug into.

After the planes bombed and left, soldiers were faced with the unenviable and massive task of going to places that had been struck to clear debris of all sizes, assemble the dead and gather body parts that were unceremoniously strewn over wide areas. We knew what the soldiers had to do, though we were not allowed to accompany them. The pervasive atmosphere was as overpowering as it was unsettling.

There was the day when my mother and Mrs Victoria Aguiyi-

Ironsi, wife of the late head of state, were at the Umuahia market when it became the target of an air attack. It was a harrowing experience that left wanton and widespread destruction of property and lives. For those who survived but lost limbs and pieces of flesh and bone, perhaps death would have been a more merciful option. Fortunately, and incredibly, my mother and Mrs Aguiyi-Ironsi emerged unscathed. But the wife (and, I believe, the child) of one Dr Nkele, family friends, were not so lucky; they died in the carnage resulting from a separate attack. We were fortunate that our camp was not hit throughout the time we lived there. It wasn't because we had sophisticated weapons with which to deter the enemy. It was just luck.

Things ultimately deteriorated into a mischievously sadistic game where harmless refugee camps, hospitals, schools, residential areas and markets were rocketed and bombed from the sky. Although I didn't witness it, I recall the intriguing tale of a young girl who had been buried by a bomb blast but was alive when she was eventually exhumed. There was also much excitement when the ceramics industry was hit. We visited the scene shortly after and observed the crater that had formed in front of the large building. Fortunately, it hadn't been a direct hit.

Mr Sam Nwoye, one of my father's aides and Secretary to the Biafran Militia, lived across from us with his family. Standing beside his home was one of several mango trees that dotted the camp. This one was especially noticeable because it produced enormous fruit that we called *German mangoes*. When one of them turned yellow, an indication that it had ripened, the temptation to pluck and eat it was too strong and worth taking any risk to achieve the goal. Instead of bringing it down with stones and sticks, I thought climbing up the tree would be a quicker and more effective way to reach and harvest the prize. It was a tall tree and I knew that the climb would require extra effort. But I also welcomed the challenge.

I was close to my destination when, from nowhere, I heard a sudden but unmistakable deafening sound. It was the terrifying arrival of an enemy plane that had come to drop bombs on Umuahia. As was common, the plane had lost a lot of height and was flying low so that the delivery of its devastating package could be achieved effortlessly. The mango tree was near the edge of a valley across which the plane glided confidently as if aware that Biafra lacked the basic weaponry with which to thwart its attack. I thought I could see the pilot's head and for a brief moment, even if fabricated in my mind, he seemed to look at me with a smirk that implied unapologetic disdain.

I was stunned but not panicked. After all, we were now accustomed to the sights and sounds of bombers that arrived and departed uninvited. There was no time to climb down the tree and I didn't think twice about letting go of the branch that would otherwise have provided the final bridge to my much-anticipated *German mango*. Despite the considerable height, I didn't feel any pains when I landed and in seconds was racing to the bomb shelter in which members of my family were already huddled.

Even when the air was at peace, war was everywhere. At strategic points within, around, and on the fringes of the camp, there were posts manned by a handful of soldiers. In general, too, soldiers always milled around, especially around the dormitories that they occupied. Behind our home, overlooking the valley, was a rocket-launcher station that was always guarded by two or three soldiers. The launcher was a simple pipe-like contraption on which a rocket was mounted. The rocket would be launched when two wires, which were connected to the rocket, were placed against the positive and negative ends of a car battery. I know of only one instance when it was used. On that day, we huddled in a bunker as an enemy plane cruised over Umuahia, occasionally dropping bombs in the indiscriminate manner that was routine. In the distance, the sounds of gunfire and other explosives indicated that Biafran soldiers were fervently trying to either bring down the plane or at least scare it away. And then, without warning, a blast sounded all too close and much louder than the rest. Instinctively, we all cringed; my initial thought was that the enemy plane had scored a direct hit on our compound, the house perhaps. Not long after, the plane left and we emerged from the underground shelter to learn that a rocket had been fired at the plane from behind our house. It explained the extra loud blast.

Then we saw God and he smiled at us. With the terrifying air raids, it was a welcome relief when 30 May arrived and we celebrated Biafra's one-year anniversary in a colourful parade. We treasured the moment as it briefly threw a veil over the beast that was closing in on us each day. And yet it was a simple affair best illustrated by the modest booths built with sticks and palm fronds at one end of the large field where the spectacle took place. It was from here that we, the spectators, watched as soldiers marched past a dais where Ojukwu stood and received their salute. Standing on both sides of the dais were Biafra's leading military personnel.

After the parade, and on a more humorous note, the head of state joined a group of soldiers to subdue a cow that would be slaughtered for the ensuing entertainments. As they yanked the rope tied to the ill-fated animal's neck, for that moment, if not at other times, the Biafran leader displayed himself as a man of the people. Before we got home that day we briefly dropped in at the State House for reasons that were not clear to me, for it was indeed a brief stopover. But it was another extraordinary opportunity to behold the bearded head of state up close. He stepped out from an inner room carrying a glass of something that he sipped. After acknowledging our greetings with a smile and a few words, he disappeared and so did we.

The war was a masculine thing – the marching soldiers, the guns and the bombs. At least that's what we believed. So, Victor formed a mini all-boys army and recruited me, my brothers and other boys who lived within the camp and the neighbourhood. We organized parades, recces and football matches. I remember one of those recces when we happened upon a pack of monkeys that scampered into a valley and out of sight once they spotted us. Naturally, Victor was the supreme commander and, while I don't remember who had what rank, I recall that I rose to the impressive rank of captain. We were tough; my macho nickname was Scorpion Dagger.

The more we interacted with the soldiers, the more they told us battle stories, took us through the stages of military parades and convinced us that ours was a righteous and gallant army up against a cowardly and evil enemy that would soon be defeated. We eventually made special friends among the soldiers. Charles's friend was a sergeant whom we simply called Sarge. Mine was a dark, hefty private that smiled a lot. His name was Ubani. Ubani didn't only tell me lots of stories, he took me on long walks. I asked him many questions about the war, the battlefronts, hopes of victory and weapons. I remember the day he took me on a walk outside the camp. We reached a track that led down to a stream that rested at the bottom of a valley and, because I was too scared to walk down the track, Ubani picked me up on his shoulder and walked halfway down before walking back up. I remember because this was my last encounter with him.

There was another soldier. Though he wasn't anyone's special friend he was a sight to behold, and therefore worthy of our attention. He was somewhere between sixty and sixty-five at the time. I am not sure if it was because he was old, but his uniform was always rumpled, baggy and not too clean. He must have enlisted with a serious desire to fight for the Biafran cause, but I think he ended up playing more of a comic-relief role. We called him Baba Uwa, Father of the World. His antics became well known around the camp and must have been accepted as a much-needed digression from fear and danger, to humour and spectacle. No one bothered him as he walked around, usually in his bare feet or in rubber slippers, spreading wisecracks and looking for things to do. One of his favourite pastimes was collecting old aluminium cans and fashioning them into cooking pots.

We owe our soldier friends much gratitude for being a lively distraction at a time when we no longer saw or interacted with our environment in a way children usually do. We also seemed to be mocked by a presence that was determined to taint any grain of leisure we discovered. Either that or we became too comfortable with the soldiers and increasingly flirted with the risky behavior that dominated their fantastic stories. They seemed to want us to take the risks, which might explain why they gave us some degree of freedom to play with their rifles. On this particular day, Valentine was visiting one of the soldiers in his room. I don't recall who the man was; it may have been Corporal Uchendu, Lance Corporal Sampson, or another soldier whom we called Dead Body. Anyway, Valentine had stripped the soldier's Sub Machine Carbine (SMC) and put it back together quite skillfully. He then cocked the weapon and inserted a loaded magazine into it. Just then I walked into the room and Valentine, with his finger on the trigger, playfully pointed the rifle at me. Alarmed, I protested and quickly stepped aside. To my astonishment, and the soldier's, Valentine actually pulled the trigger. The rifle let out a loud bang, spitting out a bullet that missed me by inches and lodged in the wall in front of Valentine. Was he trying to kill me? Just happy to be alive, I didn't care to know the answer. Of course Valentine had not tried to kill me, but even if what I know now had been explained to me back then, at my age I wouldn't have understood. With more recent clarification from my other brother, Charles, it all makes sense to me. Valentine's behavior that day was based on what he had been made to believe about an AK-47, true or false. Supposedly, if an AK-47 was cocked before a loaded magazine was attached to it, there would be no discharge when its trigger was pulled. For a bullet to enter its firing chamber, a magazine had to be inserted before cocking the weapon. Because he assumed the SMC's mechanism was similar, he also assumed the rifle couldn't be fired, even if it carried a loaded magazine. He had, after all, cocked the weapon before inserting the magazine. Though he was proven wrong, we were all relieved that the bullet had lodged in the wall and not in any part of my body.

Our friendship with the soldiers led to other unusual incidents. Charles developed whooping cough in Umuahia, causing him much discomfort. Each time he coughed, he made a whooping sound and threw up. In time, I too contracted the illness and suffered the same fate, which became a dilemma in the face of scarce and ineffective medication. One day, a soldier called us aside and convinced us that he had a cure for the cough.

"Don't tell your mother or father," he cautioned us.

"We won't tell," we promised, eager to learn about this magic solution to our distressing problem.

"I will boil lizard and you will drink the water," he explained.

We agreed without question.

Witnin a few days, we were in the soldier's room where we drank the seasoned water in which he had boiled some lizards. The cough didn't go but at least we didn't die. In fact, the cough wouldn't go until the war was almost over. Charles and I kept our secret, especially from my mother.

Perhaps we had put our faith in the lizard broth because we were aware that lizards were becoming a regular dietary supplement for an increasing number of displaced and destitute Biafrans. Privileged as we were, we never starved and neither did thousands of other Biafrans who otherwise would have, thanks to the sheer industry of those who never lost their lands, as well as the philanthropy of the Red Cross and other Christian groups and NGOs. Not to mention the compassion of people like the Irish, who were not deterred by their distance from Biafra, or the risks and difficulties that it took to provide us with relief. But even privilege was of no consequence when it came to foodstuff like ordinary bread, sugar and milk, which soon became luxuries that eluded everyone, including us. More delightful treats like cornflakes, ice cream, soft drinks, biscuits and cakes ceased to exist completely, and I came to forget what they tasted like until after the war.

It was soon evident that Biafra was not only fighting a war against bombs, bullets and grenades, but against starvation. The signs were gradual, but soon gained momentum, becoming glaring and ruthless. At first the soldiers were fed three times a day. Then it was cut to twice. Before we left Umuahia, they received only one meal a day. When the local children dug around for *abuzu* – crickets – we thought it was an exciting pastime, especially when a large cricket was unearthed from its underground home – we joined in. Led by our nature-curious cousin, Sonny, I became an expert at identifying the tell-tale mounds that marked a cricket's home and perfected the art of digging it out alive within a short time. After they were captured, we played with them, feeding the crickets leaves, but eventually eating them. First we'd clean out their insides and spice them with salt and red pepper; then we'd roast or fry them. This was an exciting sport for me and my brothers, but for many others it was done out of hunger and in an effort to supplement shrinking meals. One day we intervened after we spotted two children hunting for grasshoppers in the valley behind our home. Because the smelly green and yellow creatures were almost stationary as they clung to the shrubs that they nibbled on, it was easy for the children to catch and store them in plastic bags. We invited the young hunters to the compound and handed them a few fingers of plantain. They thanked us, but, as they walked off, still held tightly to the bags that contained their grasshoppers.

The truth became more apparent as the once well-fed soldiers became more experimental with their meals. The hibiscus leaf was famously used as a vegetable substitute for preparing soups and was considered a major success in this regard. Where beef, erstwhile an important part of lunch and dinner, was not easily accessible, rodents of every kind and forest animals, either trapped or killed with local rifles, became a tasty addition to meals. Sometimes, *achara,* the thick stem of a special shrub, became the creative replacement for beef, even in our home. Other plants, grasshoppers and an assortment of creatures, big or small, were eventually added to the menu of many Biafrans. There are those who swear that human flesh was on the list too.

Food was not the only thing that became scarce. Blackouts were so frequent that the presence of light bulbs almost caused suspicion. Pipe-borne water began to dry up until it ceased altogether. For days, the toilets remained unflushed so that it became more conducive to use surrounding bushes. Regrettably, the bushes seemed to be used for that purpose by everyone else too, especially the soldiers, and one had to be careful where you stepped. We got creative and this took some of the degradation out of the situation, like when we climbed trees and *aimed* from there or simply deposited *it* between the branches.

We were still at Umuahia when we had to face one of the saddest episodes of the war. On a hot afternoon, soldiers posted to our home at Ikot Ekpene began to straggle into the camp, exhausted, disheartened and injured. One of them was my father's younger brother, Etim, who at that time was a sergeant in the Biafran Army. They recounted horrific stories of how the enemy had finally captured Ikot Ekpene and how they had escaped and made the thirty-two-mile trip to Umuahia on foot, navigating secret bush routes, perhaps with the assistance of villagers. One of the stories they told is still as confusing as it was troubling. At one point the soldiers ran into a vigilante checkpoint mounted at one of the villages. The vigilantes set out to interrogate them in Igbo. Because my uncle couldn't speak Igbo, he was immediately suspected of being a captured Nigerian soldier. It was enough reason for the vigilantes to demand that the other soldiers hand him over to them. They planned to kill him. It took a lot of explaining and appeals for the villagers to be convinced that Etim was indeed a Biafran soldier and, more importantly, that he was my father's younger brother. It made sense. If the second-highest ranking Biafran was not Igbo, then some Biafran soldiers could equally be non-Igbos. The truth is that thousands of Biafran soldiers were not Igbos and fought until the bitter end in their undying efforts at protecting the young nation. The incident is a reminder of how deep-seated the ethnic tensions and intolerance had become.

Because of its unique position, the fall of Ikot Ekpene was crucial to Biafra's eventual defeat. Once Nigerian soldiers were able to overrun the town, they had fairly easy access to major Biafran cities, particularly Umuahia to the northwest and Aba to the southwest, and thus the heart of Biafra. Later, when they eventually marched into these cities, Biafra's collapse was imminent. It is therefore important to recap the process of advance on, and capture of, Ikot Ekpene, which would have lasting consequences for the town, Biafra, and my family.

For me to have clear memories of this collapse would not be possible at my tender age and my recollection necessarily borrows from accounts eyewitnessed by relatives and friends, not least being my uncle, Isong, who still lives in Ikot Ekpene.

Ironically, the advance in July 1968, which originated in Calabar to the east, was led by an indigene of the town, Colonel Edet Akpan Utuk. He therefore had the advantage of knowing the terrain and of devising the most strategic means to enter the town with minimal notice. Colonel Utuk was also a nephew of my father's stepmother, *Eka Etim* (Mother of Etim), which made him our in-law. The first member of our family to realize that federal troops were descending on the town was my uncle, Edet, who was on his way to his grandmother's house at 88 Umuahia Road (the same highway on which our family home stood), where he was usually guaranteed a meal. But before Edet arrived there, he noticed that people were fleeing in his direction – back into Ikot Ekpene's centre. On inquiry, he learned that Nigerian soldiers had arrived and were making inroads into the town. Edet ran back to our family compound at 55 Umuahia Road and informed the soldiers on duty of the situation. The soldiers immediately passed the news to my father who was in the compound at the time. Though his initial reaction was to secure reinforcement from Umuahia, he sent five soldiers to investigate the situation and report back to him. Rumour has it the men ran into Nigerian soldiers at a place called Ikot Atasung and fled for their lives, never returning to report back. Unsure of what had happened to the soldiers, my father assessed the situation as urgent enough for him to move family members to the safety of Umuahia and directed that a car be made available for that purpose. The car left with his mother, his stepmother (Eka Etim) and our cousin, Ime, who was in her pre- or early teens. Ime was Small Papa's daughter and oldest child. Because Umuahia Road was already sealed off by Nigerian soldiers, they had to take the longer way via Aba Road. Grandfather would have been one of the passengers if he had not gone to the village of Nyaranyin to take care of a patient. After the car left, my father departed to Aba as part of his quest for Biafran soldiers who could confront the enemy at Ikot Ekpene. He also planned to secure and send another vehicle to bring other relatives from Ikot Ekpene to Umuahia. Meanwhile, his younger brother, Etim and four other soldiers stayed behind at the family compound.

As the encroaching Nigerian soldiers penetrated Ikot Ekpene, several of the local people sought favour with them by pointing out our family home. It was, after all, the prized home of none other than Major General Efiong, General Ojukwu's second-in-command. Among the informants were neighbours, presumed friends, and one of the Nigerian soldiers, Private Edet Udo Udiong Ukpe, who was also an indigene of Ikot Ekpene. The soldiers intensified their gunfire and sped up their advance with hopes of capturing Biafra's number two man. They finally arrived at our compound where they killed Iyaro, a family friend who was visiting and was from Benin. There are those who theorize that he was mistaken for the Biafran leader, Ojukwu, because of his bushy beard.

Etim tried to escape through the back bushes but ran into Nigerian soldiers who arrested him. Fortunately, the man who led the assault, Colonel Utuk, was his cousin. This was obviously unbeknown to the Nigerian soldiers otherwise they might, understandably, have been suspicious of Etim's escape shortly thereafter. As they marched forward, Utuk appeared from the rear with his captured cousin. The colonel then pushed Etim into the bush, gesturing for him to run away as he started shooting in a different direction. This gave Etim enough time to escape as the ruse sent the Nigerian soldiers scampering in the wrong direction in search of him. Etim eventually met up with the other guards and together they made the long trek to Umuahia through remote villages and bush tracks.

Fortunately for Edet, one of the Nigerian officers, Lieutenant Colonel John Ariyo, took him under his care and ensured his safety until the end of the war. Ariyo had served with my father in the Second Battalion at Abeokuta before this war.

Not all members of our household were as fortunate as Etim and Edet. Grandfather had since returned from Nyaranyin and was in the compound when the Nigerian soldiers arrived. Also in the compound were Small Papa and Eyo, my father's long-time cook, all of whom were identified by what had become a growing and frenzied mob. The soldiers appreciated the disclosure, as would a hunter who had finally routed an elusive beast. None of this made sense to me as I had come to regard Ikot Ekpene as home and its people as my people. But this was a war and I came to understand that people would do whatever it took to survive, even if this meant currying favour from an adversary they had only recently described as evil.

Eyo was conscripted into the Nigerian army and later died under mysterious circumstances. Women and children of the family were generally spared major physical injury. Some had fled or went into hiding in surrounding bushes before the enemy reached our compound. Small Papa was given a severe beating, to the point of almost mutilating one of his eyes. He later lost his vision in that eye and, before his death in 2005, became totally blind. Though Grandfather was not handled as ruthlessly, he was still roughed up while his hands and feet were bound. He was then forced to watch Nigerian soldiers blow up our main house and the other homes occupied by relatives within the compound. But first, the soldiers, neighbours and those whom we had recently considered friends, had a field day looting the house, stripping it bare.

Small Papa's soap and gin factory, which provided employment to several residents of Ikot Ekpene, was also demolished after it was pointed out to the Nigerian soldiers. Although the factory would almost certainly have been destroyed, one contention is that its fate was sealed because of a grudge that Private Ukpe held against our family. His father, Mr Udiong Ukpe, was supposedly involved in a land dispute with Grandfather over 61 Umuahia Road, which is where the factory was built.

Grandfather and Small Papa were later released and, together with other relatives, made their way to our village, Ikot Akpan Obong in Ibiono, about fourteen miles away, where they found refuge. At the end of the war, we learned about the death of three of these relatives: Grandfather, Small Papa's wife – a kind and gentle woman whom we called *Eka Comfort* (Mother of Comfort) – and Small Papa's youngest child, Asuquo, who was the same age as my younger brother Francis. They all died from a combination of conditions brought on by the war – hunger, poor health and grief.

Meanwhile, Grandmother and Eka Etim settled down to a fairly constant routine of resting, taking walks and occasionally doing light chores at Umuahia. Ime, with time, became preoccupied with domestic work, mostly taking care of Francis. Grandmother's customary role of disciplinarian shifted in response to the violent threats that the war unleashed. Her words of caution, as if rehearsed, became repetitive and therefore predictable, reminding us of the need to be alert to potential air attacks.

"Keep the noise down and open your ears," She would interject in Ibibio, "so that we would hear when an enemy plane arrives!"

She repeated these words so frequently that they became commonplace without necessarily losing their seriousness, evolving into something of a ritual chant that warned us of the need to remain vigilant and not get carried away by a youthful exuberance that could easily overlook the terror that increasingly embraced us. Eka Etim may have had a tougher time resettling in Umuahia, since she was leaving behind an active schedule and socially fulfilling lifestyle that involved ample peer interaction, trading and communal safety. For her, therefore, an inconsistent routine at Umuahia resulted in what must have been dreary and even depressing.

A day after Grandmother, Eka Etim and Ime arrived at Umuahia, my father, who was still in Aba, sent a Land Rover to bring more of our relatives to Umuahia. But the enemy had already taken control of Ikot Ekpene and, close to our family compound, the Land Rover ran into an ambush. One of the escorts was killed while the driver and other escorts escaped, making their way back to Umuahia from Ikot Ekpene on foot. It was they who apprised my parents of the incident and I listened in as I usually did throughout the crisis when friends, relatives, strangers and military aides delivered demoralising stories. I was, and still am, devastated by the terrible news that the escort killed was none other than my special soldier-friend, Ubani. The reality of the war hit me hardest at this point.

I missed Ubani dearly. I still miss him.

Soldiers were sometimes put through gruelling disciplinary routines that involved the frog jump, rolling from one end of a field to another, or receiving several lashes with a cane. After all, Biafra was all business and had little patience for unruly or insubordinate soldiers. But it wasn't insubordination that led to the disciplining of one of the soldiers assigned to our home. It was an accusation of theft: stealing a can of tobacco. Although I can't recall his name, I remember him to be tall, slim and gentle. My father smoked, but he didn't chew tobacco. Still, there had to be a reason why the case was serious enough for him to get involved. Maybe it was his mother who chewed the leaves, or maybe they were ground into snuff for her. Anyway, I watched in the living room as my father interrogated this soldier about the can of tobacco. Despite his repeated insistence that he was innocent, he was found guilty and sent out to one of the battlefields as punishment. In a few weeks, this same soldier returned to the camp and paid us a visit. He was his jovial self and chatted playfully with Charles and me as if he had never left. This was puzzling since the man had every reason to be resentful and bitter. After all, he had lost almost half of one arm at the warfront, probably to a grenade. He occasionally looked at the bandaged stump and quietly swore at the person who he claimed had falsely accused him of stealing the tobacco.

Chapter 5

The Promised Land, without milk or honey

Because the air attacks on Umuahia were so rampant and terrifying, my father became worried and, for our safety, decided to relocate us to Umudike, a town on the outskirts of Umuahia, about seven miles away. Umudike could be described as semi-urban, quiet and self-contained, without the busyness of the larger towns and cities. We settled in a holiday-type caravan that stood beside a spacious wooden bungalow practically erected on stilts. The bungalow was occupied by family friends – Doctor Akpabio, a well-known physician, his Jamaican wife, Aunty Daphne and some of their relatives. To deal with the problem of space in the caravan, Rosalyn and Mercy slept in the wooden house at night, as did Eka Etim, Grandmother and our cousin, Ime. We all relied on the bathroom facilities in the house. Otherwise, my mother, me, Charles, Valentine and Francis all squeezed into the caravan, which had a single bedroom, a living room area and a kitchenette. My mother shared the bedroom with Francis while my older brothers and I made do with the built-in settees in the living room. Behind the main house was a smaller building for the domestic help, which is where Akataka, our cook, was quartered with one or two soldier aides.

Though there was no space to conduct a makeshift school, my mother still engaged the services of a teacher to instruct us in whatever creative way she imagined. I recall that she did little more than teach us songs and lead us through various games. One of her favourites was to have us create a circle in which we safeguarded a 'goat' played by a chosen pupil, while every effort was made to keep a 'leopard', played by another pupil, out of the circle. If the 'leopard' managed to bulldoze its way into the circle, the 'goat' was let out, while the 'leopard' was then caged. The highlight of the game was when the 'leopard' escaped the circle and chased after the 'goat', which it usually caught while we cheered excitedly. Throughout the game, we sang a simple song in Igbo that I still remember.

Onye ekwela ka agu bata, agu ga-egbu ewu.
No one should allow the leopard to come in, the leopard will kill the goat.

There were other families in the area that we knew, though I am not sure if they were in Umudike for safety reasons like we were. They didn't live far away and we occasionally visited them. Andrew and Yvette, the children of Brigadier Anthony Eze, were much younger than us, which explains why we didn't spend any significant time at their home. We spent more time with Ukpong and Ifiok, the sons of Mr Akpan Ekukinam-Bassey, who were close in age to Valentine and Charles. Though he was a civilian lawyer before the war, Ekukinam-Bassey rose to the rank of colonel in Biafra's militia. On one visit to his home, I remember that Ukpong gave me a ride on a small motorcycle. Though it was only a short ride, I don't know how I could have accepted and trusted that motorcycle ride. Ukpong was about twelve years old.

We explored Umudike in other ways and it offered the serenity that my father had hoped for. One of our favourite pastimes was to visit the roadside collection of large cages in which monkeys were held. We didn't know why the cages were displayed on the side of the road or who owned them. But none of that mattered. To us, they were a free and rare spectacle and we took advantage, visiting them quite often and sometimes feeding them bananas or other snacks.

When we weren't up and about the roads of Umudike, we entertained ourselves at home. Two of Dr. Akpabio's relatives were boys whom we occasionally visited. Though they were relatively young, they were skilled at building card castles. It was the first time that we witnessed this unusual skill and the main reason we enjoyed their company.

A few rubber trees straddled an area behind the building where the house staff stayed. With the help of one of the soldiers, we one day decided to use a knife or similar sharp object to cut into the side of the largest tree. A sap began to trickle out and we patiently tapped and rolled it into a small ball in what was quite a lengthy process. Sometimes we took breaks to eat or attend to other chores, after which we returned to creating and shaping the ball. After some days, the ball reached a reasonable size and we used it to play football and other creative games.

Not far from the caravan was a guava tree that we assaulted frequently for its fruit. As should be expected, we went for the guavas that weren't too high because they were easier to reach and pluck. But after depleting the low-hanging fruit, we realized that accessing guavas on the higher branches would not be that easy. We tried to bring them down with missiles that came in the form of sticks and stones. But the missiles didn't bring them down quickly enough or in sufficient numbers. To resolve the problem, one afternoon I decided to climb the tree and grab the elusive guavas. All seemed to go well until I got to a point and realized that I simply couldn't climb any higher. The problem was that I also couldn't find my way back down. I was stuck. I stayed in that position for a while until I decided to swallow my pride and began to scream, "I'm stuck, and I can't come down!" It didn't take long for my mother and brothers to hear and trace my cry to the base of the tree, as did some of the occupants of the main house. Their first reaction was to laugh and make fun of me. Most embarrassing was that Father Isidore Umanah was visiting at the time. Apart from being a family friend, he was instrumental in organizing relief for Biafran refugees and was also the principal of my secondary school, Holy Family College, after the war. Known for his undying sense of humour, he contributed to the jokes that were being hurled at me. My plight ended after two soldiers were instructed to climb up the guava tree and bring me down.

Though my appetite for guavas declined significantly, I still climbed trees, even though I was conscious of not climbing too high. I climbed them in a daily ritual that reminded me that we were in a ferocious war, notwithstanding the relative calm of Umudike. Almost every late afternoon, in a large field behind the caravan, Biafran amputees gathered to play football. I climbed a tree to watch them. The matches were quite competitive and, for players who used crutches because most of them had lost a leg or part thereof, they played with unparalelled energy that I struggled to comprehend. It was another pointer to the stubborn faith that Biafrans held onto.

Throughout the time we spent at Umudike, we didn't experience a single air attack, which is what my father had hoped for. But he had to cut short our stay and return us to Umuahia rather unceremoniously. The enemy was quickly bearing down on the city and my father wanted us to be with him when they arrived.

I missed Umudike, but the image of amputee football players stayed with me.

We returned to Umuahia and soon witnessed one of the most theatrical incidents of the war. News had reached my father that one of the neighbours that had vandalized and looted our home at Ikot Ekpene was spotted at a refugee camp. A plot was hatched and an impostor, acting as a government official, was sent to inform the man, whom we came to know as Udiong, that he could be transferred to a refugee camp that had better food and healthcare services. The old man, who was Grandfather's peer, fell for the ploy. He was transported from the camp and deposited at the entrance to our camp. News of his arrival reached us and we gathered at the top of the road from where we witnessed his slow ascent, escorted by one or two soldiers. He was tying a wrapper and covered his torso with a vest or T-shirt. One of Udiong's legs was slightly crooked, which slowed his walk considerably. He carried an old suitcase on his head, one that he had looted from our home and supported it with a long flexible cane with which he used to clamp it down. Finally, Udiong arrived. He was thin and fragile and understandably exhausted and apprehensive. I remember his bulging eyes, his wrinkles and his inability to say much. He was ordered to place the suitcase on the ground and open it. He complied and my father searched through it. All kinds of items were discovered in there, most of which belonged to us. Among them were my father's clothing and several family photographs. My father asked Udiong several questions throughout the encounter and passed sarcastic comments about how the thief had done a good job of looting our things but was stupid enough to fall for the ruse that had brought him to Umuahia. Udiong was finally handed back the suitcase and its entire contents, after which my father ordered that he be detained in the camp guardroom. We tagged along as soldiers escorted him back down the road to the dormitory rooms, one of which served as the guardroom. They jeered at the decrepit old thief and were not bashful about making the most sacrilegious comments. Someone even commented that he would have been chopped up and roasted, but for the fact that his meat would be poisonous and taste nasty. During the next few days, we periodically stopped by at the guardroom to check on Udiong, whose door was left wide open except at night. He was a terrified wreck and emaciated quickly. Keeping him there was really of no use unless he was to be executed. Within a few days, he was released.

I later learned that Udiong was the man who'd had a land dispute with Grandfather and whose son had helped direct Nigerian soldiers to our home and my uncle's soap factory at Ikot Ekpene, which were ransacked and demolished.

After the war I saw Udiong once when we attended mass at Saint Vincent de Paul Church in Ikot Ekpene. I particularly remember how tufts of hair stuck out of his ears. At the time, we were visiting Ikot Ekpene where we went on occasional trips from Enugu, our new dwelling place. Our Ikot Ekpene home had been rebuilt, but it was merely a shadow of its old self since the new structure was really a mud home coated with whitewash. Udiong didn't show any animosity towards my family, unless he carried out a masterful suppression of his feelings. I am also not aware that his larger family made any attempts to get even with us. But when I think of Udiong, I feel nothing but great pity.

Despite the war, there were moments of consolation. One day, a family friend, Uncle Modu, gave my mother a small cassette player-recorder, the first we ever owned or saw. It reintroduced a semblance of technology, much of which had been lost to the war. It was also a rallying point for regaining hints of laughter, mischief and awe; for the magic of recording and toying with one's voice was indeed magic. My mother's older sister, Mama Nkechi, seized the moment and we watched in fascination as my mother recorded her songs each time she visited. They were mainly Biafran songs that were fast gaining ground as a tool for comfort and inspiration and a means of expressing sadness, fear and hope. While some of them were sung in English, the majority were in Igbo. They were sung in different situations, at all kinds of gatherings: when we worked, when we relaxed and when soldiers marched. Collectively created and owned, they soon became household items. I learned and sang some of those songs, both in English and Igbo. I remember one of Mama Nkechi's favourites:

Ojukwu bu eze Biafra,
Edere ya na Aburi,
Awolowo, Yakubu Gowon
Unu enweghi ike imeri Biafra,
Biafra win the war!
Amodu car, shelling machine, heavy artillery
Boom!

Ojukwu is the leader of Biafra
This was written at Aburi,
Awolowo, Yakubu Gowon
You cannot defeat Biafra,

Biafra win the war!
Armoured car, shelling machine, heavy artillery
Boom!

Next to Mama Nkechi, Francis amused us by frequently reciting poems and songs into the tape recorder. For him, it had to be a welcome digression from the growing, senseless madness.

Such was the fantasy that we wrapped ourselves in amid so much turbulence, to the extent that we once attended a traditional dance – my first – and I remember how one of the young female dancers won over my heart. In the escapism the dances offered was the promise of survival; it was tangible and underscored the fact that there was a yearning across Biafra; a yearning that surpassed status or class and found a reason to laugh amid so much ugliness and uncertainty. It was a yearning that must have been the motivation for those who ran a cinema theatre in Umuahia, despite crumbling infrastructure. I mostly slept through a movie we watched there one night, though I enjoyed the strange outing.

We even found time, one afternoon, to go on a half-hour or so drive from Umuahia to a place overlaid with foliage and friendly trees. Aside from me and my siblings, there were other friends of the family, mainly friends of my older sisters. Within this large area of unusual serenity, we played and rediscovered laughter. Before dark we returned to Umuahia and to the mockery of war. It was eerie how we were accompanied by the ghost of war, even as we tried to invent normalcy.

Returning from somewhere one afternoon with my brothers and sisters, we were almost all killed. On this day, our car headed towards a railway crossing as a train sped towards it. But, like a lot of mechanical things in Biafra, the warning signal at the crossing was not working. There was bound to be a collision if a pedestrian hadn't yelled out and alerted us to the oncoming locomotive. The driver slammed on his brakes and our lives were spared.

But luck was not on the side of a little boy on that day when Nnanna, my father's main driver, was taking me back to the house, perhaps from the clinic at my father's office. There was a slight drizzle and a few children stood at the roadside waiting for an opportunity to cross. They carried pots, pans and basins on their heads, all of which were covered with banana leaves to protect their contents from the drizzle. We weren't driving too fast, but we were fast enough not to be able to stop in time when one of the children suddenly dashed across the road. Nnanna hit the brakes but still ran into the boy who couldn't have been older than me. We cleared to the side of the road where things happened fast. The boy's friends or siblings – whatever the other children were to him – immediately went into loud lamentation as he lay still on the side of the road. The banana leaves with which he had covered his container littered the area around him. I took one glance back at the child and then looked ahead, unable to deal with the gruesome scenario. In a matter of seconds, a crowd assembled with people reacting differently. Some grieved, some were alarmed and some offered suggestions on how to save him; that is, if he wasn't yet dead. Our green military car and the fact that Nnanna was wearing his army uniform might have secured our safety, for it is not unusual for cars, drivers and passengers to be lynched and torched in situations like that. The chaos soon died down after the boy was lifted into a van and driven off – to a hospital, I hope. I don't know if he survived. We drove off shortly thereafter and arrived at the camp without incident. I wasn't eager to share the experience with anyone.

It was one thing for a boy to be hit by a car during war, rather than a prospective bullet or other missile. It was quite another for a man to lose his precious car. Even more disheartening was that the loss resulted from sheer carelessness at a time when ownership of any form of property was increasingly rare and relished with a fervour that was almost cultic. The day was without incident until we were jolted by a rumbling sound, which was uncanny as it wasn't the rumbling of military hardware or ammunition. My brothers and I rushed out in time to catch a glimpse of a car plummeting down a valley behind a family home that stood about a hundred yards from ours at the far end of the camp. The car was increasingly torn to pieces as it gained momentum until what was left of it finally settled at the bottom of the valley. It is not clear what human error caused the accident, not that it mattered to the owner of the little black car who couldn't hide his anguish and wept aloud. I had never seen a man shed such massive amounts of tears. To lose something whose value more than quadrupled because of the war is beyond comprehension, as is the agony it must have caused. But we now had a reason to periodically explore the bottom of the valley where the wreckage lay. We looked at it, imagined what led to its fate, played inside it, but soon lost interest after it was systematically stripped until little or nothing was left of the vehicle.

A different type of thrill unfolded on another day when gunfire and other explosions sounded all through Umuahia and drowned out the sound of anything else. We panicked and scampered to nowhere in particular, but didn't seek shelter in the bunkers because this, after all, was not an air attack. We eventually huddled in an area in front of the house as the commotion continued. After about thirty or forty minutes, the sounds died down, and then, just as quickly as they had begun, news spread. Russia had allegedly recognized Biafra. My mother began to rejoice and do a mini dance when my father barked at her to be quiet. He knew that it could have been a false rumour and indeed that's what it turned out to be. But the incident was troubling enough to generate new anxieties. In response, my father went on to improve security by stationing more soldiers at strategic positions around the camp.

In a rather bizarre and even masochistic way, the crisis hit home one evening when a family friend entertained us with a movie projector that flashed images on our living room wall. The Charlie Chaplain sketches were an immediate hit, but they were brief and the hilarity was quickly replaced when the room was filled with more dominant images capturing the gory massacre and repatriation of easterners from the north before the war. Years later I reflected on the real tragedy of this horror story, the fact that even though the victims were described as easterners, mainly Igbos, in reality many of them were northerners in terms of what they ate, their clothing, language and lifestyle. My maternal grandmother is a constant reminder of this bitter truth. Though she was Ukwuani, an ethnic group in the western Niger Delta with significant linguistic and cultural ties to Igbos, she had spent several years in the north where she thrived as a property owner in Sabon Gari in Zaria. Although her late British husband had helped her purchase the rooms she rented out, she also traded in various food items and was therefore self-sufficient and had all she needed to raise and provide for her four children as a single parent. When easterners were violently expelled from the north, my grandmother lost her real estate business that had taken her many years to establish. But at least she didn't lose her life. Like my mother and her brothers and sister, the north was the birthplace of many easterners who were attacked and brutally driven out of that part of Nigeria. They had been raised there. Some could not even speak Igbo or the language of their ancestral homes. Instead, they spoke the dominant Hausa language of the north fluently. They were butchered by their kith and kin, fellow workers, neighbours, friends and so-called loved ones. They were slaughtered by people with whom they shared communities and with whom they had entered into business. They were not strangers that had been destroyed and exiled from a foreign land. The film was a gory re-enactment of blood, mutilation and death.

Fortunately, after the war my grandmother's son, Uncle Joe, was able to travel to the north, reclaim her property and sell it, bringing the proceeds back to his mother. Sadly, many easterners would never recover their homes and businesses because they were either destroyed or seized by their former neighbours.

Though the movie projector reminded us that we were at war, another event was to foreshadow our last stand at Umuahia. It began with a family visit to a relief centre run by reverend sisters somewhere outside the city. I can't remember how many of us went with my mother, but I recall another woman with a child who ate like a pig. I found him annoying even though the grownups were amused by his gluttony and laughed out loud. Looking back, I know the boy should not be blamed, for even we, as privileged as we were, had long given up on the type of snacks that the reverend sisters offered. Bread had become as elusive as the yeti and biscuits even more so. Yet, the reverend sisters could afford a reasonable supply of these and other goodies, including powdered milk and *chin-chin* – a fried delicacy comprising flour, sugar and butter – which were all part of the relief consignment that ended up in refugee camps and other feeding centres.

By evening, we thanked the sisters for their hospitality, bade them farewell and began the drive back, which was uneventful until we got to the outskirts of Umuahia. What we ran into was as scary as it was startling. A huge crowd of men, women and children were surging out of the city in our direction, lugging as much as they could, from pots and pans to mats and rickety furniture. Earlier, travelling that same route, it was relatively calm and as empty as one would expect a highway at wartime. We were therefore mystified by the madness that suddenly descended on us. Parents carried children that were too small to walk; the women mostly strapped them to their backs with cloth. It was quite unsettling that we were obviously approaching whatever danger they were running from. Soldiers mingled with the crowd; they were hostile and tried to beat them back with their rifles, boots, sticks, or bare hands. This didn't make sense to me since the people were apparently running from something that terrified them. In retrospect, I can only imagine the deep sense of insecurity and failure that the soldiers were desperately trying to conceal. The rushing exodus of people from Umuahia was a reminder, after all, that the Biafran soldiers had failed to prevent the enemy from advancing on the city.

Finally, we arrived at home, though I was still plagued by uncertainty about the newfound horror that was forcing this large exodus out of the city. Things happened quickly.

Chapter 6

Banished from our blue paradise

The next morning, we understood that we had to immediately relocate. A lorry with a roofless rear arrived from somewhere and things were hurled into it with an urgency that was almost hysterical and in no particular sequence: clothing, boxes, furniture, pots and pans. The soldiers, house staff and the rest of us, joined in what became something of a gothic carnival. Mama Nkechi and her five children were also on hand to be transported out of Umuahia and participated in 'loading' the lorry. The frenzy came to a climax when the building behind the main house was broken into. Immediately, all attention shifted to this building as we set out to loot it. The news soon spread and people from all over the camp, soldiers and civilians alike, descended on the building, ransacking it and helping themselves to all kinds of things. The news reached Reverend Jason Onuoha, the caretaker of the Institute, who came to see things for himself. He arrived, hobbling on one leg as he always did, took one look at the mayhem, turned around and headed back down the pathway that led to his home, visibly distraught. He must have accepted the inevitable, that he had lost all control of safety of the Institute and its possessions.

There was only so much that the lorry could hold and once full we departed. My father stayed behind while the rest of us squeezed into two cars; some of the military and civilian aids shared the front of the lorry with the driver. Mama Nkechi's young servant, Simon, was the only one who didn't enjoy the comfort of a roofed vehicle. He rode on the back of the lorry amid all that we had piled up there. If anyone knew our destination, I certainly had no clue. We zigzagged for about two hours, mostly through back roads.

Finally, we arrived at Ifakala, essentially a large village that didn't even have the commercial appearance of Ikot Ekpene. But nestled within its rural innocence and simple homes was the compound that accommodated an impressive two-story building, which was our final stop. It was the home of Chief Iregbulem, the father of my father's first aide-de-camp, Hilary Iregbulem. We must have been sudden intruders on the Iregbulem property, as there couldn't have been enough time to negotiate our arrival and sojourn there. But I doubt that our entrance caused little more than expected curiosity. The sudden appearance of homeless relatives and strangers seeking shelter and food had become customary in Biafra. If agreements were reached on where and how we would reside at the compound, they were probably done by Hilary and his father.

Chief Iregbulem was extremely gracious, generous, patient and kind. He offered us the choice of either occupying the top or bottom level of his home. My mother opted for the top level. It had about four rooms, a veranda, a toilet, a bathroom and a kitchen. It was an unusually comfortable arrangement for Biafra, although it lacked the grandeur of the Central Bible Institute and the sense of independence and authority that we had enjoyed there. We were after all squatters and would have been freeloaders too had we not prepared our own meals. But the change in environment and the sense of loss didn't discourage me as they once had. In a silent, undetectable yet effective way, the war was equipping me with an immunity that was as psychological as it was psychosomatic, forcing me to accept and live with the constant deviation from what should have been standard and comfortable. I also knew, despite being young, that we still enjoyed the type of privilege that many Biafrans had long ceased to hope for, even in our newfound state of dependency and homelessness.

My mother and Mama Nkechi occupied one of the bedrooms in the Iregbulem home, which they shared with my younger brother Francis and Mama Nkechi's youngest child Chidozie, whom we called Doe. Grandmother and Eka Etim occupied another room, while the rest of us boys and girls were divided into the remaining two rooms where we shared the few mattresses that had been hauled from Umuahia. Because they were only a handful, some of us had to sleep on raffia mats that were spread on the floor at night. The room in which Grandmother and Eka Etim stayed was adjacent to the room occupied by us, the boys. At night, when we knew the old women were settling down to sleep, we lay on the floor and used our heels to bang on the wall that separated our room from theirs. Ignoring their loud complaints, we didn't stop, not until my mother or Mama Nkechi intervened and warned or smacked us. Undeterred, we committed the same crime repeatedly, refusing to give up on a sadistic source of entertainment. After all, there was very little else to do. Sleep was not something to slump into; we looked forward to it with excitement as it was a time to laugh, tell stories, wrestle and stamp on the wall to exasperate Grandmother and Eka Etim. Pre-war pastimes, which no longer existed, had to be replaced.

Food time was marked by its own brand of expectation, with meals doled out to mealtime partners of two or three, who ate from a single plate. Years later, I understood that this arrangement was a psychological strategy my mother had invented. Because food was in short supply, piling up what appeared to be a large amount on a single plate looked generous and concealed the truth about shortages. Separated onto two or three plates the woefully inadequate portions would have been all too apparent. The ploy was successful and after every meal we smacked our lips in contentment. Notwithstanding the strategy, thousands of Biafrans would have relished a fraction of what we enjoyed.

We increasingly relied on relief that Biafran sympathizers were sneaking in from nations like the Ivory Coast, Gabon, Ireland, São Tomé and Tanzania. The Catholic Church, the Red Cross, Caritas and other Christian groups were also at the forefront of bringing in and distributing food, medication and clothing. Even *garri*, erstwhile an everyday and inexpensive staple, had become inaccessible and where available, was no longer affordable. It was widely replaced by what we all called *Formula Two*, a wheat-based flour product that was mixed into a paste with hot water and eaten in a variety of ways, including, like *garri*, with any of several vegetable sauces. stockfish, or *okporoko* as it was widely called, entered Biafra in large quantities and became a major dietary supplement, quickly replacing meat and sometimes prepared alone. Mainly supplied by Norway, it was regular fish that was preserved by being butterflied and air-dried without salt. There was another brand of preserved fish that was delivered to Biafra too. Not as popular as stockfish, this one was super-salted and undried. Popularly called Saltfish, it had to be washed thoroughly, otherwise, it would introduce too much salt into any meal. In time, it became a good source of salt, which had become scarce. Corned beef, rice, powdered milk and powdered egg (a unique regimen processed from egg yolk), were also among the assortment of foods that charitable organizations and supportive nations delivered to Biafra, sometimes at great risk.

One of the large rooms on the ground floor of the Iregbulem home was used to store relief supplies. Some agreement had apparently been reached between the family and some or other charity. A caretaker ran the place and supervised the distribution of relief to the refugee camps. One morning, we woke up and received the news that thieves had raided the store. The iron bars that safeguarded its window were twisted apart until room was created for the thieves to enter and remove some items. Fortunately, despite being twisted, the bars still presented an obstacle and prevented the thieves from taking too much. Though the caretaker, who slept in the store, was apprehended, tied up and whipped, he was not seriously injured and displayed just a few bruises. Otherwise, there was no real threat to our peaceful stay at the Iregbulem compound.

Food variety dropped and I got tired of eating the same thing repeatedly, or of eating new meals like *Formula Two* whose taste I could never quite get used too. Sometimes I simply refused to eat and preferred something less standard but more familiar and palatable, like *garri* soaked in water and mixed with powdered milk and groundnuts. I wasn't the only occasional mealtime dissenter; my mother always yelled about how things were difficult and how we didn't appreciate that we had much more than most people. She was right but we were children.

With the collapse of Biafra's infrastructure, occasional trips had to be made to a large body of water, perhaps a tributary of a prominent river, to wash clothes or fetch water that was rationed and used for cooking, drinking and bathing. I once accompanied the fetchers and washers to the river, not to help out but to explore a new play setting. That day, I ran along the banks of the river and frolicked in the shallows. The short water supply also meant that we had to use the bucket latrine cubicles that were housed in a modest building on the fringes of the Iregbulem compound. I accepted them rather dispassionately and they didn't offend like they once had at Spencer Street and Ikot Ekpene.

At night, Chief Iregbulem's generator lit up the compound. This was unprecedented, even miraculous, since such opulence contrasted strikingly with the scarcity that surrounded us. It was a huge machine with a lever that had to be wound with considerable strength before it came to life and was the first that I had ever seen.

Aside from the building that we stayed in, there were other smaller buildings within the compound, which were occupied by relatives and most likely a few other squatters like us. Among Chief Iregbulem's children, I have vivid memories of the twins, Peter and Paul and another son, Kiriam. Although they kept their distance they remained friendly, as if to mind their business while allowing us to mind ours. There was no doubt, however, about their cordiality and generosity. Hilary, the oldest, breezed in and out, but didn't live there. He was a Biafran officer with a posting outside Ifakala. Whenever he visited, his girlfriend also showed up. Even at my age I thought she was dainty and cheerful, but I hated the fact that she teased me about being her husband and sometimes tried to grab me as if to truly express her affection. Each time, I struggled and escaped.

We all found different ways to adjust to Ifakala. Grandmother and Eka Etim kept each other company, took occasional walks

AN Barracks, Yaba, Lagos, around 1960. This bungalow is 18 AN Barracks, the home of former Regimental Sergeant Major Robert Millington of the Nigerian Army Royal Army Ordnance Corps (RAOC). Our home was at number 34. (Photo courtesy of Peter Millington)

My younger brother Francis, Umuahia, 1967/68. More than any of us, he was perhaps most distressed by the war, eventually surviving bouts of anxiety and confusion, as well as an attack of cerebrospinal meningitis. In the background is a bunker/bomb shelter.

Held by my mother, Josephine Efiong (née Abbott), Kaduna 1961. I am wearing a dress because my mother hoped that I would be a girl and prepared for the arrival of a daughter.

My father and mother, Umuahia 1967/68.

A worn and much-thumbed photograph of us at Ikot Ekpene 1967. Front, left to right: Francis, my younger brother on the tricycle, Nneka, my cousin, and Charles, my older brother. I am right behind Nneka, slightly hidden. Behind, left to right: Nkechi, my cousin and Mercy, my older sister. The house in the background was blown up during the War.

Umuahia showing a camouflaged house in the background. Others in the photo are my father, my two older sisters, my younger brother (in the car) and my father's aide-de-camp stepping out of the building.

Umuahia, 1967/68. Front, left to right: Charles, Valentine, Francis, me. Behind, left to right: Mercy and Rosalyn.

2 Hyde Park Gardens in Blackrock, Dublin, Ireland, where Charles and I stayed with the O'Connell family after the war. (Photo courtesy of Declan O'Connell)

Bouaké, Ivory Coast, 1970 after the war. Left to right: me, my younger brother Francis, and my older brother Charles.

Dublin, 1970, after the war, on a visit to the Murphy home where my older brother and sisters stayed. Behind, left to right: Mr Murphy, Moira, Mrs Murphy, and Gearoid. Front, left to right: Mercy, me, Valentine, Charles and Rosalyn.

Charles (left) and I on summer vacation at the Aran Islands with the O'Connell family.

Attending a conference on Biafra at the University of Galway in Ireland, 2011, where I reunited with Moira Murphy after 41 years

The house on Spencer Street in Lagos where my family was given refuge by the Trimnell family after we fled AN Barracks following the second coup of July 1966. Sadly, the home has suffered depreciation over the years. (Image courtesy of Angela Ehrlich née Trimnell)

Cover page of Biafran passport owned by Mr Ignatius Kogbara, Biafran Ambassador to the United Kingdom. (Photo courtesy of Donu Kogbara)

Front pages of Biafran passport owned by Mr Ignatius Kogbara, Biafran Ambassador to the United Kingdom. (Photo courtesy of Donu Kogbara)

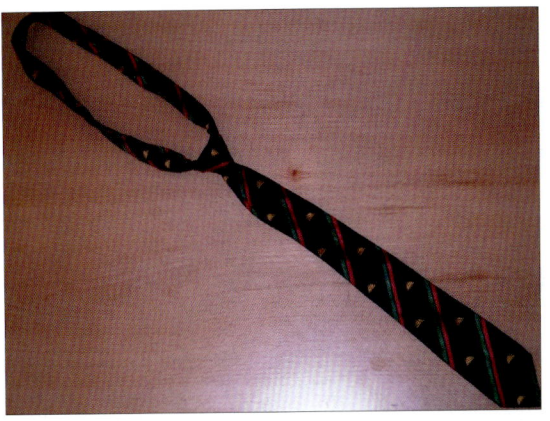

Personal Biafran Necktie.

Insignia of the Biafra Air Force.
(Image Courtesy of Ken Conboy)

Shoulder insignias of Biafran Army officers.
(Image courtesy of Ken Conboy)

A Biafran scarf retrieved from our family
compound in Ikot Ekpene, 2005.

The Biafra Sun: this emblem was worn on the upper arm of military uniforms. (Image Courtesy of Ken Conboy)

The hat my father used as a Biafran General, retrieved from the family compound in Ikot Ekpene, 2005.

A ticket for a music and video programme organized to raise funds for Biafra at the Foxrock Folk Club in Ireland, November 1969. (Photo courtesy of Jeremy Kearney) around the compound, ate, slept and admonished us, mainly the boys, for being mischievous and playing practical jokes.

Valentine mostly explored Ifakala alone, or in the company of Victor. Charles, Sonny (Victor's younger brother) and I formed a clique that searched out Ifakala as widely as was possible under the circumstances. Rosalyn and Mercy, being ardent readers, found enough time to read and reread books that they owned before the war started. When they socialized, it was mainly with the older Iregbulem children and Victor. Ime, our cousin and Mama Nkechi's older daughter, Nkechi, spent more time at home than anywhere else, often performing a variety of simple chores. Mama Nkechi's two youngest children, Nneka and Chidozie, kept each other company. While my mother took special care of Francis, who was about three and very reserved, along with Mama Nkechi she managed the home and kept a close eye on all of us.

When we first arrived at Ifakala, the primary school across the street from the Iregbulem home was still in session. In the mornings we could see the students in their khaki uniforms being organized for the day's activities before they sang and marched into their various classes. Later, they took their lunch break during which they played, laughed and ate their snacks as if in defiance of the prevalent gloom. But within a few weeks the school shut abruptly. Like other schools in Biafra this one could not be sustained and was also needed to house the growing number of refugees who kept arriving from places that had been overrun by Nigerian soldiers.

When we went to school in Ifakala we didn't attend the one across the road from us, although we used one of its empty classrooms. My mother made special arrangements for Charles,

Sonny and I to receive private evening lessons from a teacher, perhaps one that used to teach in the school. Because the teacher's name was so unique I remember it well: Longinus Dimuna. His lessons were straightforward and rich, easygoing and hardly strenuous. Though he usually prepared lessons for Sonny and I that were different from what was assigned to Charles, on several occasions we all received the same lessons in mathematics, spellings, history and Igbo songs. A cordial relationship developed between us and Mr Dimuna such that one day he had us over to his home where his wife served us *jollof* rice and corned beef. I remember clearly that she was very heavy with child.

The highlight of our brief academic experience in Ifakala, however, did not come with Mr Dimuna's teachings; it came with the teachings of a man who, for whatever reason, saw himself as an educator and great orator. He mostly foraged through the school compound and surrounding bushes and perhaps slept in one of the classrooms at night. I remember him to be tall, slim and dark, usually wearing what looked like a bluish caftan. Sometimes, when Mr Dimuna arrived late for classes or didn't show up at all, this man would saunter into our classroom from one of the side doors. Because we had become used to crazed war victims wandering around Ifakala we weren't afraid of him, or surprised by his presence. He actually stirred our curiosity and in time we became fascinated by him. This was partly because he spoke so eloquently; his English was impeccable, producing a glaring incompatibility with his appearance. His lectures were always the same; he recounted the interesting story of Julius Caesar and whenever he reached the end of his narrative evoked the Roman Emperor's murder in theatrical fashion, quoting

Caesar's final words: '*Et tu Brute!*' We ultimately came to know him as *Et tu Brutus*. While he may have been one of several Biafrans whose senses had been defaced by the war and replaced by delusions, it is not inconceivable that he was a respected teacher, perhaps university lecturer, prior to the war.

For unknown reasons our classes with Mr Dimuna also ended unexpectedly. We were not surprised and I really didn't care. Not long after, the classrooms were occupied by refugees.

Mama Nkechi was concerned about Sonny, who, among all her children, she thought was lacking in academic promise. On certain evenings she would hold him down and force him to read from a children's storybook. Each time he misread, or couldn't read a word, she handed out a slap across his cheek or a knock on his head. Sonny always wailed aloud, but his mother was relentless, as if she were determined to pound knowledge into his head with her knuckles. The rest of us just watched as if grateful that we were 'too smart' to be subjected to such torture. Sometimes, in his agony and desperation, Sonny escaped his mother's grip and ran for dear life. But it was to no avail as Victor always went after him and shortly after Sonny was returned to their mother. (Today, Sonny is a successful businessman. His mother was apparently wrong about his intellectual aptitude and he should be laughing at many of us who do not enjoy anything close to his success. But he is gracious.)

Before the school across the road was converted into a refugee camp, one already existed a short distance away which we occasionally visited. Six-spring beds, mattresses and raffia mats were arranged inside its three or four buildings for occupants that comprised the old, the young, family members and orphans. The oldest and youngest were the most vulnerable, the most famished, the most frightened and the most tormented. The camp carried a peculiar smell, a combination of unwashed bodies and of unwashed clothes, of sickness, of hunger, of urine and of defecation. Without any toilet facilities, surrounding bushes served that purpose. On one of our visits we watched as something boiled in a cauldron. Food for the refugees, it seemed, but closer inspection revealed blankets steaming in the huge pot. It was the only way to eliminate anything unsanitary from the blankets, including bedbugs and lice.

In its desolation, the camp remained active. Malnourished children sauntered around on spindly legs with distended stomachs, huge heads and bulging eyes. From my brother, Valentine, we learned that some of them discharged a strange liquid from their bodies. One day he returned home with stories of a starving girl whose state of decay forced a smelly liquid to ooze down her legs. He recounted details of the spectacle with gestures that were meant to evoke its torment and repulsion. With each piece of his account, he reached down below his knees and feigned scooping up and flicking away streams of a contaminated fluid. It was not until after the war that I learned that kwashiorkor, Biafra's widespread hunger syndrome, was not an Igbo word. Studies suggest that the name is derived from Ga, a Ghanian coastal language, and refers to the sickness that a baby is inflicted with after birth, or the disease of a child apparently deposed by a newborn sibling. This belief is an interesting reevaluation of sibling rivalry. Though this form of severe protein malnutrition has been well documented around the world throughout history, its prevalence among populations that made up Biafra was new and therefore very strange. The disfigurations it brought on the human body and mind were alarming.

My first encounter with a starving child on mosquito legs with a distended stomach was not relayed through my brother or a curious witness. It happened during one of our early visits to the refugee camp. The child was stark naked and I could tell that he was a boy, though his penis was almost completely concealed by his stomach. He frightened me. For someone who was about five, parts of his dark skin were more wrinkled than they should have been. I couldn't make sense of how his legs were able to carry his massive head and stomach. But that wasn't the only miracle. A lady walked up to him and asked in Igbo, '*i choro milik?*' She pronounced milk, *milik,* most likely the same way the child would have pronounced the priceless drink. He nodded and the lady mixed a few spoons of powdered milk in a cup of water and handed it to him. He drank and I became more frightened because I didn't understand how his stomach could accommodate anything else, as distended as it already was. But he drank the entire cup of powdered milk and with each gulp I cringed, expecting his stomach to explode.

With a heavy shortage of medicines, food and water, this camp, like many others was a storehouse of imaginary hope and death was a frequent guest. Whenever someone died, we ran to the camp to witness the lamentations, as was the case when a mother mourned the loss of her young son. Sitting on the same bed on which the corpse lay, she wailed until she no longer had tears. Every now and then she paused and called out to her dead child. If she expected him to respond, it wasn't surprising since his eyes were still open, giving the impression that he stared at the ceiling. But he didn't. We didn't wait for his burial.

In the evening of a different day news of another death reached us from the camp that was once a school. We rushed to the site and observed the latter stage of an unceremonious funeral where several refugees, young and old, openly expressed their grief with tears and jarring cries. A grave was hurriedly dug in front of a former classroom and shortly after a dead child was laid in it. Before he was covered with earth, rags were placed on top of him. Sacred funeral procedures had long been abandoned in Biafra and every piece of earth was considered suitable burial ground.

Although we rushed out to see things each time someone died, the deaths did not come as a shock, not even as a surprise. We were curious about them, but hardly daunted or troubled by them. Our curiosity could be compared to the type one experiences when a child takes its first steps, or perhaps the fifth time the child walks. It is not momentous, merely entertaining.

But it was not the accumulation of death, odour, sickness, despair, or even filth that was most outstanding about the camps; it was the will to persevere under the most agonizing circumstances. It didn't matter that the kwashiorkor patients increased each day and the diseases steadily secured its grip. In the evenings the refugees chanted home-grown war songs that expressed grief, but also courage and strength. Accompanied by music sprung from pieces of wood, stones, cans, bottles, pots and buckets, the sounds drifted to our compound and we frequently strolled to the camps to watch them make merry in the most solemn state, dancing in circles with energy that could only have been divine. They embodied the immortality of the Biafran dream, notwithstanding the brutal uncertainty of their situation. No matter how much the camps and their destitute occupants deteriorated in appearance, in health, hygiene and spirit, the refugees revived and emboldened themselves with music, song and dance. Restoring and relying on the ancestral sacredness of these art forms, they were able to hold onto something that couldn't be broken by disease, bombs, starvation or death.

Even when the refugees selected a song that was elegiac and didn't convey much promise, they sang with a liveliness that created confidence. I recall this one:

Nnem amutala'm
Kpo'm soja di ni me ohia
Anwunta atagbuo la nu soja'm-o
Iworiwo
A nam akwa niwe
A nam akwa niwe
Onye agbaji kwalam okpukpu
Dead body ewe nne we nna
Oga ni me ohia ga biri
Anwunta atagbuo la nu soja'm-o
Iworiwo

My mother gave birth to me
And declared me a soldier in the bush
Mosquitoes have bitten my soldier-o
Iworiwo
I am crying sorrowfully
I am crying sorrowfully
No one should break my bones

> Dead body doesn't have a mother or father
> And goes to live in the bush
> Mosquitoes have bitten my soldier-o
> *Iworiwo*

Just as the songs underlined the will to survive, so did the news of a birth, which spread with the same energy as the news of a death. Because it happened in the refugee camp that was across the road from us, it was easy to dash down there and see the mother cuddling her infant as in any normal situation. For the most part people just stared, perhaps trying to reconcile the birth in the prevailing aura of death. Ime later sneaked some of our clothes to the woman as gifts for her baby, even if they were too big for the child. Not that it mattered, since owning clothes had become the exception and not the rule. Years later, after the war, I pondered the fate of that child and the circumstances leading to its birth, not least being the steps towards conception in the cramped refugee camp or surrounding bushes. I also wondered about the absence of any man standing in as father.

The refugees remained faithful and occasionally their faith was justified, like the early afternoon when a small white van carrying a few men arrived in the old school compound across the road. One of them used a loudspeaker to call on everyone to come and receive their vaccination. If the invitation was for the refugees alone, the announcer didn't say. So there was a general drift in the direction of the compound. Everyone wanted to take advantage of whatever medical magic the men brought with them, especially since medication had all but disappeared from Biafra. In the excitement my mother sent us to participate in the exercise. A gun-shaped instrument affixed with needles was used to deliver the shots on our upper arms.

The pain was excruciating; to this day I don't know the purpose of that vaccination. If it prevented anything, it certainly didn't prevent the war from going on. It also did nothing to reverse the truth that basic medication was in short supply. We were therefore thankful that we weren't assailed by any of the grave diseases that roamed without restraint. This is despite my being afflicted a second time by what everyone believed to be measles, which I am told, is medically impossible. My first affliction had been at Ikot Ekpene about a year earlier. A few weeks after our arrival at Ifakala my skin began to develop what were now familiar and irritating bumps that gradually grew and spread until I was draped in them. Because they looked and felt like measles, they were identified and treated as such. Mama Nkechi, our impromptu physician, used an old yet effective method. At intervals during the next few days, she rinsed her mouth with palm-wine and sprayed it all over my naked body in full view of everyone. Not long after, the sores and discomfort disappeared.

When the toes of her son, Chidozie, were invaded by the larvae of flies that had burrowed into them, causing myiasis, Mama Nkechi again stepped forward, this time as surgeon. Using a razor blade she sliced through the infected toes with mysterious precision, ignoring Chidozie's agonizing yelps. The larvae were exposed and squirmed as they were swatted with a slipper or other weapon.

One of the Iregbulem twins, Peter or John, was the focus of another medical wonder. He had been diagnosed with malaria and none of the familiar quinine drugs were available, not even in the section of the building where relief supplies were stored. Without any signs of improvement in his condition, relatives familiar with age-old methods of healing immediately went to work. They gathered special herbs and roots from surrounding bushes and boiled them in a metal cauldron. The sick twin was then ushered onto a low stool next to where the cauldron was placed on the ground, still steaming hot. A small crowd gathered as a blanket was placed over the twin and the cauldron. He remained there for about five minutes after which the blanket was lifted from his body. Drenched in sweat, he was gently guided to an inner room to get much-needed rest. In a day or two he was fully recovered.

Though the refugee camps were a temporary safe house for many, space was insufficient and they were almost always overcrowded. Among the destitute, therefore, were several men, women and children – from the incredibly young to the very old – who couldn't be accommodated. But even where space was available, some of them didn't trust the comfort of the camps, or were simply not welcomed there for any number of reasons. In the end, whether their absence from the camps was forced or voluntary, they were reminders that faces of dejection and loss were not restricted to the camps.

I remember a shrunken orphan boy, somewhere between five and seven years, who roamed around half-naked, begging for something to eat; or the other beggar, perhaps in his teens, whose walk was rickety; his face carried a permanent grimace and his words were barely audible. But we managed to understand him when he listed, in Igbo, the foods that he was in desperate need of. He usually began by asking for stockfish and corn, before drifting off into an inventory that became increasingly muffled. His problem was more than hunger as his mind was evidently afflicted and no longer capable of clear and rational thought.

Even so, it was still more intact than that of the shell-shocked soldiers who occasionally hobbled to nowhere in particular. His walk was straighter than theirs too.

Shell-shocked soldiers were called artillery, or, more light-heartedly, *atimgbo*, because their condition was allegedly the result of being too close to a loud explosion at the warfront. The blast, whatever caused it, apparently did more than damage their ability to hear or maintain proper balance; it also did considerable damage to their brains. Although the common view was that their disorder was temporary, this didn't seem to reassure friends and family members who were in no hurry to lay claim to any of the *atimgbo*, so they came across as nomadic adult orphans. Their army uniforms steadily gave in to wear and tear and in time, as the fallen soldiers grew pitifully aimless, they became threadbare. When they spoke, they did so with great effort, yelling to hear themselves and stuttering for long periods before coming to a sudden halt. They didn't make much sense, whether they stuttered or not, and seemed to draw their words from a pool of ideas and images manufactured in a world of intense illusion. The shell-shocked soldiers became a common sight and were not a distraction, nuisance, threat, or cause for anxiety, just another product of this war, a sad one. Their inadvertent antics and itinerant lifestyle were a bid to survive, not to disturb. Abandoned to their mental and physical deformities, they roamed to nowhere in particular, their destinations as unpredictable as their destinies.

Conscriptions were frequent in Ifakala, a sign that Biafra was growing anxious. When this happened, a band of armed

Biafran soldiers showed up unexpectedly and invaded homes and surrounding bushes, looking to capture and recruit boys and men who bolted off in every direction. A soldier once got into a fierce argument with the marauding recruiters over their attempt to conscript his elderly father. That he was a soldier himself must have prevented him from being beaten up, just as it eventually led to the release of his father. Sometimes news spread about the impending arrival of the recruiters and all potential conscripts went into hiding. At other times the soldiers arrived before the news spread and though several men and boys escaped amid the mayhem, others were captured. As they were marched off or carted away in waiting vehicles a crowd of onlookers watched: wives, mothers, children and friends of the new conscripts, many of whom wept aloud. There was, after all, little guarantee that any of the conscripts would ever be seen again.

Though we couldn't avoid misery, we tried. We tried by exploring Ifakala. During one of our expeditions around the community we stopped at a neighbour's compound, as we often did. The well-to-do Iregbulems were known throughout the community and it didn't take long for us, their guests, to be known and accepted by the people. On this afternoon, there wasn't much activity at the compound beyond talk, but we were contented and relaxed. The mood changed, however, when the unmistakable figure of an emaciated and exhausted old woman in tattered clothing ambled into the yard. From the way the residents questioned her, she was unknown in the area and perhaps had journeyed from a distant community. The woman explained that her house had collapsed and that she needed a place to stay. Ignoring hints of an unwillingness to take her in, she went on to lie down on a palm bamboo bed that stood in an open porch. Because this is the same porch where we gathered to chitchat about the war, superstitions and anything that roused curiosity, her presence remained a permanent distraction, though we tried hard to ignore her.

That this woman was alone and uncared for indicated that she may have lost her children to the war, or they were out fighting. She may also have been cut off from relatives, which happened after the enemy occupied and isolated a region that would otherwise be crisscrossed by family members. And, if she couldn't benefit from the collective custom of building and rebuilding rural homes, it was a pointer to what people were more preoccupied with. Although her nakedness was partially visible when she first walked in, it was more exposed when she lay down. I couldn't have been the only one who noticed. She was indifferent to what she exposed.

But even away from the surrounding community the adventures continued in the Iregbulem compound and we were rarely bored. We hunted for bats. It was just another indication of how nutritionally creative Biafrans had become. Bats may have been a delicacy before the war, but hunting them increased because of hunger. Some nights they emerged from a section of the ceiling and glided to another section, sometimes in groups, sometimes alone. When this happened, the Iregbulems and the rest of us gathered in the area where the bats performed their back-and-forth flight. With weapons ranging from brooms to rags and items of clothing, they were intercepted mid-air and brought down. Each captured bat was then beheaded, sliced open, and disembowelled. Their emptied stomachs were salted and filled with pepper and other spices before they were roasted over open flames. Although I tasted this meat just once, I remember it being delicious. Sadly, even this luxury of finding food in unusual places had been deprived the likes of the half-naked women.

Sometimes, we explored outside Ifakala. But we couldn't escape the smell of war. I am not sure why, but one day we drove to a hospital some distance away. One or two military aides were with us, including my mother and Mama Nkechi, though I cannot recall who else came along. Perhaps news had reached my mother that a family member or friend had been admitted to the hospital. On the other hand, she may have been making a routine trip to visit and encourage the patients, most of whom suffered a range of wartime disabilities, the same way she periodically organized the distribution of food to the warfront. Whatever it was that took us there, my spirit has walked through the faceless halls of that hospital several times since. Though dark and gloomy, the presence of sunlight seeping through window louvers introduced illumination and some lustre to the hallways. I remember the sweet, piercing antiseptic smell that mingled with an even sweeter smell of hot pepper soup. We trudged from room to room, each setting carrying the same picture and the same smell. Beds were arranged next to each other, each one wrapped in the whitest sheets that the times could offer, except for an occasional stain, either blood or some other bodily fluid, or function. These also mingled with all else that floated around, sometimes briefly eclipsing the antiseptic soup smells. But for the most part the hospital boasted a cleanliness, neatness, and fragrance that was uncharacteristic of Biafra's crumbling healthcare and refugee crisis.

Though the beds were covered in pressed sheets and preserved a uniformity that all good hospitals are known for, their occupants stole some of the decency with their faraway stares and the miscellaneous stories they told in silence. They gazed at us, and even though it was obvious that our fortunes outshone theirs, it was not with hatred or envy, but with questions and confusion. From high up in the ceiling, thick white chords were affixed to contraptions from where they were lowered to a hand or a leg (or what was left of a hand or leg), into which sharp spikes pierced. Held firmly with the strings, the spikes hoisted the limb so that it remained there, as if in mid-flight and in anticipation of a miracle. The patients mostly remained in that position, except for those who just slept or gazed, making it difficult to tell whether they were unconscious or dead.

We trudged through the hospital and thankfully the powerful smell of hot soup was restored each time a nurse strolled by carrying a tray or pushing a trolley containing the prized enamel bowls. It was restored each time a nurse leaned over to feed a feeble patient who managed to move his lips if nothing else. In their starched white uniforms, the nurses were unusually smart and clean, for even soldiers had long given up on owning decent uniforms. But, if the smells and the whiteness had temporarily transported me from the cynical embrace of war, I was transported back just before we left. A man sat on a plastic chamber pot that was placed on the floor in a corner. He must have been somewhere in his mid to late fifties and, like other patients, simply stared at nothing as his glazed eyes asked rhetorical questions and told of many horrors. The pot was clearly too little for him as his buttock cheeks drooped over each side, dry as they were. So did his testicles over the front of the pot, almost caressing the floor. But he carried no shame, not for his sagging buttocks or his loose testicles; he carried no shame, not even for his penis that rested between his testicles, frail but nearly touching the floor.

We didn't pay special attention or spend extra time with any of the patients. Either our quest for a relative or family friend had failed, or that was not our objective on that day. We left the hospital, but the man on the chamber pot stayed in my head and reminded me of the destitute old woman in tattered clothing.

Chapter 7

Sleepwalking to the beat

Ifakala was at war, though its isolation and relative silence might have fooled anyone. The air raids were not as rampant as they were in Umuahia and I don't know of any direct hits on Ifakala from Nigerian bombers. Planes occasionally whooshed in and roared past, perhaps on their way to Owerri where a battle raged between Biafran and Nigerian forces. Owerri was about a thirty-minute drive from Ifakala. It wouldn't have made sense for Ifakala to be targeted by the enemy. Though civilian populations were bombed at Umuahia, it was at least the Biafran capital and its two top men resided and kept office there. Ifakala was a village, a big village at best. A few soldiers occasionally milled around there for whatever reason, but it was by no means a warfront and did not harbour anything close to a significant military base. We didn't have a bunker in which to seek shelter; when the planes rushed in and out we screamed, panicked and ran, usually to the undergrowth behind the house. Otherwise we just crouched in a corner of the compound and watched them come and go, terrified.

With so much uncertainty we had to console ourselves and like everyone else we leaned on the war songs among many other crutches. The songs continued to express sorrow, but more than ever they provided strength and hope in their reassuring propaganda. If they originated from a place of unmentionable anguish, they finally emerged into part of everyday Biafran life. We sang them at home and at play. Sometimes a platoon of soldiers marched by our compound singing the songs, usually led by a commanding officer. One of their favourites, and mine, went like this:

Kwambelembele-o
Baby/Sisi kwambelembele
Ewe'm ego nji a nwu cigar
Kwambelembele
Enemy plane a bombu ola
Kwambelembele
Ojukwu nyem egbe ka'm gbatuo ya/ Nwanyi muru soja agbaka nwa
Kwambelembele

Kwambelembele-o
Baby/Sister kwambelembele
I don't have money to smoke cigarettes
Kwambelembele
Enemy plane has dropped its bombs
Kwambelembele
Ojukwu give me a gun to shoot it down/A woman who births a soldier is childless
Kwambelembele

When they marched, the soldiers tried hard to look confident and energized, notwithstanding their bare feet, rubber slippers, or other inadequate clothing. Their faces, sadly, could not easily mask apparent feelings of confusion, even doubt. One day the commander of one such squad visited our home and my mother received him well with food supplied by relief efforts. A few days later he brought his men to the compound and they spent a few hours camouflaging the entire building with palm fronds. Their agility and efficiency were as mysterious as they were commendable, considering that they must have been going for days without adequate meals. Even for the privileged this had now become a common state in Biafra. It was therefore good that my mother, with the help of her sister, her sister's daughter (Nkechi), Ime and the domestic help, could feed all the soldiers that afternoon, taking advantage of some of the relief supplies stored in a room in the Iregbulem home. Delighted to have a rare, satisfying meal, the soldiers were content to find a low stool or a spot on the floor of the veranda to eat their *garri* with whatever sauce had been prepared to go with it. They spoke to each other in hushed tones as if to mask their joy, but more likely to respect the presence of their commander's wife (my mother) by not coming across as loud and overexcited. Then again, it is conceivable that the good meal didn't mask the reality of the dreadful and inescapable war experience, something they knew they would be returning to in the coming days.

Throughout our stay in Ifakala I saw my father just once. It was the time when Charles and I were taken to Bishop Shanahan Memorial College in Orlu where he had set up camp. I'm not sure why only we were chosen for this trip, and though the details are vague, I recall that the camp looked dreary and quite lifeless in contrast to the grandeur of the lively military base at Umuahia where people and activity were plentiful. Perhaps this was a sign that morale was dropping fast in Biafra. My father was anything but his buoyant self, though I'm sure he was delighted to see us. After all, we were quite well despite still being tormented by whooping cough. We spent only a night with him; the next day I was happy to leave Orlu.

Unlike this trip, Rosalyn and Mercy were to undertake a different trip altogether, one that removed them from Biafra. Notwithstanding the valiant efforts of sympathetic countries and humanitarian groups, it was increasingly clear that even they were unable to meet the needs of the country's growing destitute population. For this reason they employed a new strategy, which was to start airlifting Biafrans, mostly starving and sickly children, to welcoming countries. Most of them ended up in Gabon and the Ivory Coast because of proximity, cost-efficiency and the fact that the climate and foods in these countries were much the same as we were used to. But, courtesy of Holy Ghost Fathers (a male religious congregation of the Catholic Church), some Biafrans were relocated to Ireland, mainly for the purpose of advancing their education. Rosalyn and Mercy were among them.

For the most part not much was said about my sisters' impending trip; all plans preceding the day of their departure were therefore vague. When the day arrived they left with my mother in an official army car. Two days later my mother returned without them. All I knew was that they had eventually boarded a flight that departed Biafra's only airport at Uli.

Considering that flights into and out of Biafra were done at tremendous risk, the volunteers that embarked on these flights, whether to bring in relief or evacuate refugees, deserve eternal gratitude from former Biafrans and their future generations. It is well documented that these flights were often fired on by the enemy and that at least one of them, an International Red Cross plane, was brought down on 5 June 1969, killing all passengers on board. Yet there were those charities that were relentless in their endeavours to help and stayed the course to the end of the war, driven by their consciences and principles, regardless of the very real dangers they faced. While too many Biafrans succumbed to malnutrition and disease, because of these self-sacrificing efforts, many were saved.

Soon after, we rediscovered the safety and make-believe world of Ifakala. The death of Chief Iregbulem's mother, sad as it was, temporarily steered our thoughts away from conflict and destruction, as visitors flocked to the compound during the days leading to her burial. Because the deceased had lived a long and fruitful life, custom demanded that her departure be celebrated. A constant supply of food flowed in considerable amounts as well as palm-wine and *kai-kai* (the toxic liquor brewed from palm-wine), since bottled drinks had long dried up in Biafra. The food was harvested from personal farms while the palm-wine was tapped from surrounding trees, many of which dotted Ifakala's landscape. Ifakala was one of those remote Biafran communities that hadn't yet been invaded and plundered by Nigerian soldiers. In such communities, as long as the people had their farmlands and access to large bodies of water, they continued to subsist relatively well, feeding, clothing, healing and safeguarding themselves. The poor and dispossessed in Ifakala were usually Biafrans who had to evacuate communities that had been occupied by enemy soldiers; their only option was to seek refuge in places that hadn't directly experienced the ferocity of the war, yet.

With an abundance of food and drinks at the burial service, the people sang, danced and made music with drums and anything else that could be used to improvise a beat. We watched the daily activities from the veranda on the upper level as they went on well into the night. The unusual supply of free food and drinks attracted a constant stream of 'mourners'. On the day that the deceased was finally buried, her son the chief emerged with his rifle and, standing by the graveside, fired a few shots in the air. The coffin was then lowered.

However, it was the supernatural that offered the most curious, if bizarre, diversion from death and suffering. I had long heard of ghosts but, for the first time, I was introduced to the concept of reincarnation and believed it like everyone else. In a compound not too far off, lived an *ogbanje*, a boy who proved that reincarnation was real, for he had allegedly died and been reborn several times. To end the cycle of his going and coming, a local priest was finally called to intervene. After mounting enormous pressures on the child through persistent inquiry, the priest was finally able to persuade him to disclose where his *iyi-uwa* was hidden – the mystical object that linked him to the world of the dead and by which he was empowered to keep dying and returning. The boy's *iyi-uwa* came in the form of a white pebble that was embedded in his head. After cutting open the boy's head, the priest removed the pebble and buried it after performing a rite that rendered it impotent. This ended the boy's ability to deliberately return from the dead to literally be born again. His name was Chukwu Nat and his family compound was one of the few that we occasionally visited. At a section of the compound was the spot where his *iyi-uwa* was said to have been buried. It was covered with conspicuous red earth.

One day, a full lieutenant or a captain sped down the road on a bicycle in the direction of the Iregbulem home. This was not surprising as the war had all but destroyed standard expectations of officer conduct. But his significance soared when he stopped by at the house to meet with and inform my mother that Owerri had been recaptured by Biafran soldiers. We had been aware of the battle that raged there, as the close sounds of explosions and rifle fire were all too distinct. With time, they had become the rule, not the exception. How Owerri was recaptured by Biafra cannot be rationalized. It was 1969 and Biafra was hanging by a very thin and tattered thread. The nation barely had the resources to run a government, even less to maintain an army, navy, or air force. Its existence on paper provided more psychological consolation than real protection. Confidence was at its lowest and it was only by some divine resolve that the people kept going. Be that as it may, Biafran forces had chased the enemy out of Owerri and regained control of the city.

Without a definitive capital since Umuahia's collapse, Biafra immediately adopted Owerri as its new state home, one that revived the much-needed pride that had been lost to repeated defeats. Owerri was the best of what was left of Biafra and breathed a fresh sense of life, inspiration and dignity into the ailing young nation. As Biafra's central government and military command shifted to the city, preparations were made for us to move too. Before we left Ifakala I remember how my brothers and I commented on my mother's stomach. It had added obvious weight and we playfully admonished her for guzzling too much *garri*. In truth, she was carrying my younger sister, Philippa, who was born in April the following year, three months after the war ended.

The move from Ifakala was unique because, for the first time, we were not under pressure to escape due to a threat of bombs and rockets. We could take our time and packed as much as we could. There was no glaring nostalgia as we prepared and eventually left, except that Ifakala had reintroduced the reality of war with such gory details that my perspective on this drama, and on life and death, has been permanently engraved. The images stayed with me and to this day I still carry them, not sure of how they affect me mentally. The elderly woman who straggled to a neighbour's home in raggedy clothing, mostly naked, lamenting the collapse of her house. The shell-shocked soldiers who roamed precariously to nowhere, muttering something that didn't make sense, as if they were doing a faulty sambo shuffle. The self-proclaimed teacher whose penury and ashen caftan didn't match his mastery of Shakespeare. The naked old man who sat on a chamber pot in a hospital, on his face a distant oblivious look of indifference and confusion. The frail refugee children, their spindly legs and massive heads, their swollen bellies and rusty hair. Their pleading eyes. The famished beggars of every age, the dead, the dying, the hurriedly buried corpses of children, the wailing mothers. The refugees who danced and made music, sometimes in a daze. The refugee camp smells. The images were overpowering but I wore them unknowingly because they had become normal and I had learned to live with them. Because they had replaced all other images in my head, I had no choice but to welcome them.

At Owerri we settled in a home that stood at the farthest end of what used to be Nigeria's first Shell Camp. About seventy meters from us was a smaller, though elegant, building occupied by my father's latest aide-de-camp. Our home was bounded to the left by another family home; otherwise it was surrounded by bush. Although the battle for Owerri was fierce and long, a good number of the homes at Shell Camp were still standing and had not even been scarred by bullets or explosives.

We were finally reunited with my father after spending weeks away from him at Ifakala. Because we had carefully packed our belongings this time, it was relatively easy to furnish our new home. It also helped that my father had managed to take some furniture with him during his move from Umuahia to Orlu, which he eventually transferred to Owerri. But there was no immediate solution to the absence of water and electricity. Civilian and military servants fetched water from surrounding streams and sometimes were provided an open van in which they loaded all kinds of receptacles for that purpose.

A few days after we arrived in Owerri a lorry load of soldiers arrived with Chief Iregbulem's generator from Ifakala. I don't know what agreements were reached with the chief, but I want to believe that taking possession of the prized machine was agreed mutually. It is also possible that the chief had two generators and spared one. The machine was soon brought to life and thankfully lighted up our home and our lives.

With the departure of our sisters while we were still at Ifakala, those of us who moved to Owerri were my father, mother, Valentine, Charles, me, Francis, my father's mother, his stepmother (Eka Etim) and our cousin, Ime. Mama Nkechi and her children, though they relocated to Owerri, lived about a ten-minute drive away. We paid them frequent visits, partly to explore new forms of recreation. Mama Nkechi, who never tired of being warm, generous and motherly, always gave the best of what Biafra offered, which often came in the form of simple meals. The highpoint of our visits was when we accompanied our cousins to a stream about half a mile from their home. It was at the bottom of a small valley. Although the main goal was to wash clothes and fetch bathing and drinking water, we enjoyed frolicking and swimming naked in the stream.

Just as my father's daily convoy had reduced in size, the soldier population at Shell Camp flaunted a poor imitation of what once was at the CBI camp in Umuahia. There couldn't have been more than thirty of them and they lived about a hundred meters behind us in zinc-built cubicles that could be accessed by a footpath. They had to scrape for their meals and generally displayed a demeanour that was desperate and uncertain, yet confident. My brothers and I visited their cubicles quite frequently and were soon won over by the rate at which they successfully hunted for bush-rats. Aside from partaking in their bush-rat feasts, which my mother knew nothing about, we solicited for their homemade traps and received one or two as gifts. Night after night we set the traps using bits of cassava as bait and more often than not a bush-rat fell for the bait. Unlike when we were in Ifakala and hunted rodents, frogs and bats for sport, this time we were motivated by a yearning for meat which had long ceased to be a standard part of our meals. But we were smart enough not to ask my mother to roast dead rodents for us; instead, we took them to the soldiers who were happy to do us the favour. They didn't only roast them for us, they ate them with us too.

Early one evening the soldiers were made to gather by the road leading into the camp. They matched their shorts with T-shirts or vests and were either in their bare feet or wore shoes that were clearly fatigued. One of the more athletic soldiers was in charge; he made sure that everyone was present and issued stern orders that ensured orderliness. They arranged themselves in threes and shortly after my father arrived wearing a pair of shorts, a

T-shirt and tennis shoes. The soldier in charge barked out an order and all the soldiers stood to attention as he saluted sharply. Things happened quickly; on the leader's directive the soldiers began to jog towards the gate, out of the compound and on to the road. But it wasn't the main tarred road that they used; it was a narrow dirt road. A chant was raised, fading gradually as they faded into the distance. Valentine, Charles and I followed them for a short distance and then stopped, watched and waited, knowing that they would eventually return. About half an hour later they did, still chanting. My father smiled and beckoned us to join them. We did, but there was little distance to cover and the soldiers soon jogged back into the camp and back to the area from where they had begun their run, after which my father detached himself from the group and returned to the house. The soldier in charge then carried out a few customary drills before dismissing the men.

Looking back, my father may have organized the exercise to restore vestiges of confidence to the men and perhaps himself, to show that the camp was equipped with the human and military resources that could meet the challenges posed by a conflict that was anything but civil.

The sandy road that the soldiers had jogged down ran adjacent to the camp and ascended to a point where it disappeared among trees. Compared to the main road this one was livelier and revealed a continuous flow of people who walked up and down the red track from sunup till sundown. They walked alone or in groups; men, women, girls, boys, toddlers and babies carried by their parents or older family members. In their endless march, they lugged all kinds of things – raffia mats, pots, machetes, hoes, baskets. One day, as we played at the entrance to the camp,

Ime decided to approach two young girls as they descended the road. Beyond simple greetings, I don't believe that much else was said. Ime then lifted the lid of the soot-covered pot that one of them carried on her head and briefly peeked into it. The girls were already on their way when Ime told us that the pot contained watery soup devoid of vegetables and a wretched piece of dried fish. The road and its endless to-and-fro travellers cast a dreary shadow, one that was nonetheless lifelike and seemed to capture the relentless quest that had come to depict Biafra at this stage of its existence. The decrepit load they carried, their tired clothing, their wasted shoes and feet, their dreary meals and their dark adventure; they all seemed to indicate that Biafra had reached its crossroads. But the fact that the daily movement continued amid so little, also meant that there was hope, albeit hope that defied any logic. It was this hope that kept the people moving. If everything else they were armed with was fragile and unhealthy, their faith was vibrant and filled with songs that could never be silenced.

Armed with the resolve to conquer boredom, we one day walked aimlessly down another road. There was little activity. Very few cars or people passed by, which made sense since there were few places to go to and fewer reasons to go to those places. Things changed briefly when we arrived at a building that had once housed a shoe factory. Sitting by the road in front of the gate was a Biafran soldier who stuttered violently in an effort to communicate. His tattered uniform was no longer an unfamiliar sight. He had taken off and now clenched his worn-out boots in his hands and, as he tried desperately to utter sounds, shook the boots vigorously, pointing them in the direction of the gate leading into the premises. It was the first time since we left Ifakala that we were encountering a victim of shellshock, the result of a loud explosion or bombardment, or a prolonged exposure to combat. The soldier, despite his state of disorientation, recognized the shoe factory and, believing that it was still in operation, thought he could have his boots repaired. We observed his apparent delusion and after a few minutes walked away as if he didn't exist. To us, he was an item of war, not a victim. Items of war could be human or nonhuman objects. From what we had witnessed, they either survived or crumbled. When they survived, we were inspired. When they crumbled, we observed them with a modicum of curiosity but with the understanding that every item of war had the propensity to decay and fade. It just meant that they had completed their role and made their exit from the red stage on which the macabre theatre of war was performed.

My father maintained a second army base near Holy Rosary Hospital in Emekuku, a section of Owerri. It was about a twenty-minute drive from Shell Camp. The hospital was up and running shortly after Biafra retook Owerri, thanks to the humanitarians that continued to sacrifice so much for maimed, starving and sick Biafrans. Its reconstruction was as invaluable as it was miraculous. We were periodically taken to Emekuku when my father spent several days there, but one of our visits to the hospital turned out to be an encounter with inconceivable results. On this day, a soldier-pharmacist gave me and Charles a tablespoon each of a medicine that I can still taste. Within a day or two we were cured of the whooping cough that had plagued us for a greater part of the war.

Mrs Margaret Akpan, wife of the Secretary to the Biafran Government, ran a makeshift school from her home. It was one of many in Biafra. She was assisted by a teacher who we all called Usen. I remember the home because of what looked like a mini bomb shelter that was carved into a section of the veranda in which we had our classes. Shortly after we settled in Owerri I attended the school with my older brothers along with Mrs Akpan's children: Victor, Ekamma and Néné. From a few houses away came Brigadier and Mrs Effiong Udo Okon's four children. Brigadier Okon was a member of the militia, a section of the Biafran Army that absorbed and trained civilians at the onset of the conflict. We all shared a single classroom but were somehow separated into classes that ranged from elementary one to five, or thereabouts. Modelled after our colonial British system, students, on average, were ages six to seven in elementary one and therefore about nine or ten when they reached elementary five. Because of schooling disruptions caused by the war, there wasn't a strict adherence to age and we were all assigned to different curricula based on assessed educational proficiency. Our typical day involved reading stories, solving maths problems, writing essays and telling stories.

I was in awe of Ekamma who, though a year or so younger than me, flaunted a brilliance that was quite intimidating. She spoke eloquently on most topics, whereas I remained mute except when Usen insisted that I spoke. Even so my responses or comments, nervous as I usually was, couldn't have been remotely appreciated. Ekamma's essays were just as splendid as her understanding of the many things we talked about. Convinced that I would never be as intelligent as she was, I began to develop a phobia for learning in general.

In the scheme of things, I was easily at the bottom of the intellectual ladder created by Mrs Akpan's school. Black marks, representing poor behaviour or poor academic performance and red marks, representing good behaviour or impressive academic performance, were periodically handed out. They came in the form of small, shiny, square pieces of black or red paper that were pasted beside our names, which were written on a board nailed to a section of our class wall. As I had come to expect, my name was decorated by more black than red marks. I therefore welcomed our break periods and as we played games, observed how Valentine flirted with the girls. On some evenings and weekends we returned to the Akpan and Okon section of Owerri to play with the children of both families. Although the area was about a mile and half from our home, we trekked there and back, often using shortcuts through the bush.

Aside from the Akpan and Okon children, we didn't keep many other friends. The few we had were mostly boys who also resided in Shell Camp with their families; we periodically ran into them while wandering around the area. Two of them lived next door and when they stopped by it was usually to chitchat about whatever the imagination invented, or to pluck fruit from the lemon tree that stood behind our home. We had no use for the juice but relished the white flesh that was exposed once the outer skin was sliced. When we visited their home our attention was usually diverted from them and redirected to their father who was in the habit of playing cards with his friends. Although there was nothing particularly fascinating about the games, there was enough in the antics, gusto, pompous claims and overall braggadocio of the players to keep us captivated and entertained.

Another friend was one who I recall as tall, dark and lively. Our meeting point with him was on the streets, never in his home or ours. If a character were required to promote optimism in the middle of a brutal war, this guy could not be outdone. He talked loudly, laughed a lot, cracked jokes and seemed to be without a care in the world. The highlight of his free spiritedness was his occasional swim in the camp pool that must have been abandoned for several months. The water was emerald; one can only imagine what resided in it. Yet, this fellow swam with an enthusiasm that one would expect of a lottery winner.

Notwithstanding the company we kept at Shell Camp the war stayed close and its consequences, not always conspicuous, were heavy, well felt and persistent in their influence. We occasionally visited a section of the bush not far from our home where some fresh skeletons lay, their army uniforms still glued onto them in the form of scant pieces of shredded green. They occupied opposite sides of a bush path and could have belonged to either or both warring sides. Even without flesh they conveyed a hideous message of waste. We visited them, not to lament, nor out of any perversion, but merely to pass time and include them in our daily routine of seeking entertainment.

As one entered through the gate that led to our home, it was easy to observe a grenade hanging from a tall wire fence. Put there by some unknown person, it was live since it still carried its pin, an indication that it posed a great danger. We knew, and unflinching, walked by the fence and the grenade with the indifference that comes only with madness. After all, we had also been experimenting with explosives and guns. It was our playful way of coping with the harshness of war and of creatively embracing the wisdom in joining what we apparently couldn't beat. Each time we found unused bullets around our compound or in the surrounding bushes, we used a stone or metal object to separate the slugs from the shells, after which we emptied the gunpowder on the floor and lit it with matches. The result was a dazzling glow and rushing burst that we gazed at triumphantly, pleased with our accomplishment.

We decided to make a rifle one day. Valentine took the lead and in a day or two we had affixed a metal pipe to a wooden butt carved with a knife and whatever sharp metal object we'd laid our hands on. We then poured gunpowder into the pipe and threw a lighted match into it. A radiant flame burst forth, accompanied by the usual rushing sound. About five seconds ticked by before the base of the pipe blew up in Valentine's face. We stood there for a long silent moment, wondering what went wrong. In a delayed reaction to the shock Valentine threw away the rifle and began to whimper in pain. Only then did we realize that specks of gunpowder were embedded in his face. I mostly watched as Valentine and Charles set about picking out the specks with pins and nails. We made sure our parents didn't know about the incident.

News began to spread that Valentine would be leaving Biafra to join our sisters in Ireland. The highlight of the preparations was the day my father decided to groom Valentine on how to knot a tie. I realized that boys must have worn ties more frequently in Ireland than they did in Biafra and Nigeria. The only ties I had ever been made to wear, and it wasn't often, were those phony ones that were permanently knotted and fitted with the aid of elastic bands. But the truth didn't hit me about Valentine's exit until the day arrived; for the first time Charles and I trekked to Mrs Akpan's school alone. Before we got home that afternoon

Valentine had left. I wept, but it wasn't because he had left or that I hadn't been able to wish him farewell. It was because I had lost a small hook that I hoped to use for fishing during our next visit to our cousins. While trekking home from school that day I accidentally dropped the hook on the side of a bush path and no matter how hard I tried I just couldn't find my hook. I thought its disappearance was uncanny.

Mr Akpan Ekukinam-Bassey was still Administrator of the Annang Province. Most of the Province was now firmly in the hands of the enemy, which made his position mostly ceremonial. During visits with his family in a neighbouring town, my father and mother spent time with him and his wife while Charles and I spent time with their sons, Ukpong and Ifiok, who filled us with stories about the war and much else. Francis, who was about three or four, was typically in the care of Ime and hardly a part of our big-boy world. And then Ifiok left; I wasn't sure to which country.

Ukpong was so lonely that arrangements were made for him to come and spend some time with us. He partially took on the role of big brother, left vacant by Valentine. Some days we played football in the field next to the house with improvised goalposts made of brick-sized rocks. Though Charles and I always squared up against Ukpong, we could never defeat him. This was because when the sizeable Ukpong planted himself between his goalposts, he took up every available space. The games typically ended up with Charles and I being frustrated by our inability to score against him. At other times Ukpong continued to impress us with fantastic war stories. Otherwise, he used Charles and me to parody the punishing drills that were used on unruly soldiers and would playfully 'double' us from one end of the compound to the other.

Ukpong was easy to live with except that he refused to eat relief rice delivered by charitable organisations. It meant that my mother had to prepare something else for him each time she cooked relief rice. This was the case until she decided to pull a fast one on Ukpong and one day served him relief rice but swore that it was locally grown. He lapped everything up, virtually smacking his lips. My mother waited for him to empty his plate before she broke the news. His response came in the form of an embarrassed look that remains priceless.

Chapter 8

The future was around us, bright and desolate

Biafra was alive again. As if to remind us of the fact, each time a car drove by it let out a series of loud explosions through its exhaust pipe. Biafra's refined petroleum was the culprit, but no one cared as long as it ensured that our vehicles moved. It was also an indication of the remarkable culture of creativity and innovation that Biafra had to rely on to survive and remain sane, which produced an assortment of weapons, fabrics, medicines, skin lotions and the famous Biafran tea. At the time, Biafra owned a provisional refinery that was built at Uzuakoli on land that was not normally considered oil-producing. In addition to this refinery, petroleum was produced on several other locations, from residential areas to military bases. Two drums of Biafra's refined petroleum permanently stood behind our home. Thanks to this fuel we were able to visit Father Isidore Umanah and the refugee camp that he ran at Nto Edino in present Akwa Ibom State. In relative wealth and size it was a vibrant camp and a grand, even revolutionary, departure from what I had seen at Ifakala. The buildings were spacious, the refugees were healthy and well fed and an overall aura of effective organization prevailed. The people milled around, eager it seemed, to accomplish any of several activities. The highlight of this all-round vigour came in the form of a paramilitary unit made up of boys that may have been in their pre- and early teens. There were about twenty of them and they constantly paraded around the compound in precise formation. Under the command of a sprightly lad, they flaunted a confidence that the entire Biafran Army could have borrowed from. Now and then this commander fired his homemade rifle in the air as if to warn the enemy to back off.

During the two nights we spent there we stayed in the same building occupied by Father Umanah where he served, among other dishes, stockfish pepper soup which I was tasting for the first time. When Charles and I guzzled too much my father and mother intervened firmly, apparently concerned that greed was replacing courtesy. But the supervising priest was relentless in his attempts at impressing us with his generous supply of relief and constantly referred to himself, proudly and jokingly, as 'the anti-kwashiorkor'.

The night before we left Nto Edino we had the pleasure of watching an elaborate and magnificent drama scripted and performed by the refugees. How they were able to reach inside and uncover such talent, discipline, diligence and energy is mindboggling but indicative of their determination not to be broken. To this day two lines that were constantly repeated throughout the play still resound in my head: 'Look at Annang burning. Beautiful Annang burning!' Though the play addressed the destruction and suffering caused by the war, in the end, as in the life of the people, the players squeezed out a reason to celebrate. The lively dance performance that followed immediately after was therefore appropriate. But the grand finale was the presentation of gifts to my mother and father. My mother received what looked like a large, decorated drinking glass while my father was given what may have been a local carving or wooden tray. Our trip to Nto Edino was to be our last experimentation with leisure.

The war was taking its toll on what was left of the Biafran spirit and one day the truth was served by way of my father's angry voice. It wasn't unusual for him to yell at soldiers, but in this instance he was yelling at my mother, something that I had never seen him do. I was afraid and indignant on her behalf. It was even more disheartening that she was being scolded in front of the house help and Ukpong. Regardless of the reason for my father's anger, looking back I realize that people were edgy because of growing tensions and would snap for the slightest reason.

Desperation was aggravated by widespread hunger and was the likely reason why a soldier at a checkpoint harassed and extorted relief foodstuff from my aunt, Mama Nkechi. The soldier may not have been so overambitious if he realized that she was sister-in-law to the head of state's deputy. Mama Nkechi brought the matter to the attention of my father and mother, after which a group of soldiers were sent out to arrest the culprit. That evening he was forced to lie on the ground as another soldier dealt him numerous lashes. When one cane splintered into pieces it was replaced with a new one. My father, mother, Ukpong and Charles were there to watch as the man thrashed about in agony and screamed until he could only grunt. Though I was horrified and thought the punishment was too harsh, I couldn't stop watching.

It was one thing for a low-ranking soldier to extort food but quite another for the rogue to be my father's own aide-de-camp. He had apparently been going to one of Biafra's food centres, perhaps a relief station or the Food Directorate, and was signing for the release of food on behalf of my father. He did this for a while without stirring suspicion, until the transactions came to my father's attention by way of passing conversation with an official at the facility. Investigations were carried out and once the offender was clearly identified he was marked for arrest and disciplinary action. The scandal featured prominently in common gossip and became a rare thriller at the time. I'm not sure what the aide-de-camp's ultimate fate was, but he was immediately stripped of his rank and position, kicked out of his official residence and detained. Since the house was near ours we easily observed the unhappy and humiliating process of moving out. Unfortunately, it was the fallen adjutant's wife that was dumped with the responsibility, which took a few days. On one of those days news reached us that she was being attacked by another woman, apparently one of her husband's mistresses. The story goes that he had quite a number of them. My father, some of his military and civilian aides, Charles, Ukpong and I went over to the house right away. The tormented wife was helpless and in tears, having been slapped across the face by the larger woman who strutted around the house with unconcealed authority. As we walked in she looked my father straight in the eye and demanded: 'Are you the general?' There was a moment of silence, during which no one said anything. One of the soldiers then grabbed her and tried to remove her from the house. She put up a courageous fight, struggling frantically but with little result, especially when other men joined in and forcefully threw her out. They then went ahead and gave her a sound beating as she writhed on the ground, still giving the false impression of defiance. Dishevelled and with a tattered dress, the woman was finally taken to the main gate and tossed out of the camp.

One morning, as my father was on his way to work, a man crashed into his official car with a Volkswagen Beetle. Even though it was ruled an accident, one wonders at the magnitude of the man's poor judgment, despite the convoy (though diminished) that shielded my father's car. It was as if he was trying to express his frustration at a vision that no longer had a purpose. Human error was therefore questioned and rumours soon spread that it was deliberate. We rushed to the gate where the man was being held and witnessed as he sat on a bench breathing heavily through his mouth. He was large and seemed oblivious to the combination of admonition and consolation from the soldiers. Even when some of them accused him of putting on an act and charged him with being part of a plot to kill my father, he remained unresponsive. His eyes bulged and despite the amounts of air he swallowed he looked as if he were about to suffocate. Years later I learned that this was a case of hyperventilation. While I don't know what became of that man, I felt very sorry for him that day.

But what was even more disturbing, and indicative of deepening tensions, was what we didn't see or hear. It was the guards at the gate that eventually recounted how the camp had been briefly invaded by a band of soldiers whose motive was yet to be determined. The incident had taken place in the small hours of one morning and, fortunately, the invaders were not armed, or the story might have been different. As the guards confronted the unexpected visitors, some of them were able to alert other soldiers at the camp. Although many of the intruders eventually escaped, others were subdued, arrested and detained in a military base pending further investigations. I am clueless about what those investigations uncovered. Perhaps nothing or perhaps they were never concluded, seeing that the end of the war, unbeknownst to us, was very near. I can only assume that the near-tragic events of that early morning were symptomatic of growing frustrations, uncertainties and anxieties within Biafra. People, especially children and the elderly, were dying at alarming rates predominantly due to starvation, the morale of poorly equipped and poorly fed soldiers was at its lowest, and infrastructure was all but obliterated within the ailing and tottering nation. The latter were aggravated by the illegitimacy of the Biafran currency and economic blockades that isolated us, thanks to effective economic offensives by Nigeria. It is conceivable that those who attacked our camp were protesting the Biafran Government's handling of the war and expressing their opposition to continued armed conflict. Biafra was run by a military government, which meant that demonstrations against its leadership were unlawful. In that case, the attackers resorted to what they might have believed was the only option available them. The headquarters of Ojukwu should have been their target, but they were likely deterred by his beefed-up security and went after his deputy, my father.

And yet, one of the most incredible moments of the war was still to take place; it was as extreme in its magical appeal as it was in its departure from the prevalent reality of misery, hunger and anguish. Early one evening, a huge trailer arrived unexpectedly, delivering massive amounts of food, everything from powdered egg and powdered milk, to rice and stockfish. Caught unawares, we looked on, including my mother and father who were overwhelmed and unable to hide their bewilderment and embarrassment. Even in peacetime it would have been too much food. The *gift*, the trailer driver explained, was courtesy of a Catholic bishop who supervised the distribution of relief supplies. Though appreciative, my parents' reaction indicated their unease over the sheer abundance of food in the face of excessive starvation. They immediately sent out word announcing the arrival of the trailer and its cargo and in minutes the compound was flooded with soldiers carrying bowls, pots and other containers. As contents of the trailer were doled out to them by designated colleagues, the atmosphere was one of controlled revelry.

But the soldiers didn't have time to fully enjoy the lavish treat, neither did we. In a matter of days, the enemy would re-enter and retake Owerri, forcing us to embark on our final flight.

On a trip either to or from Emekuku, I was in the car with my mother, Charles and probably Francis. Suddenly a convoy loomed in the distance, an unusual spectacle at this stage of the war. Car sales were non-existent in Biafra. Many people who owned cars before the war had to stop using them after they broke down and couldn't be fixed. Others simply couldn't find or purchase the fuel needed to operate their cars. Thus the number of cars on the roads dwindled significantly as the war progressed. The presence of a long line of cars on the highway was therefore very strange and could only mean that a top dignitary was in transit to somewhere. A man sitting next to the driver of the first vehicle extended his hand from the window. In it he carried a red flag that fluttered wildly in the wind, warning other vehicles, cyclists, motorcyclists and pedestrians to get out of the way. The head of state was approaching.

What a surprise.

Our vehicle cleared to the side of the road as the fleet of cars drove by. But then the unexpected happened. The cars slowed down, came to a halt and began to reverse. Ojukwu had apparently recognized us, or more likely the official car that we were in, and ordered the convoy to halt and drive back to where we were parked. After his orderly opened his door and saluted him smartly, he stepped out of his Mercedes, still displaying a towering figure. Although he mostly spoke to my mother, I observed him with the innocence of a child in total adoration of his eternal charisma. It was the first time I was seeing him up-close since that day, more than a year earlier, when we had briefly stopped by State House in Umuahia after attending a parade celebrating Biafra's one year anniversary.

The conversation didn't last long and His Excellency soon waved at us and got back into his official car, after which the convoy drove off and disappeared in the distance.

As we would discover in the days ahead, our chance meeting with Ojukwu was prophetic on so many levels, even ominous. He was, after all, our unbreakable leader, a status that was soon to be tested in the most flagrant and unexpected way.

Throughout our stay in Owerri, we didn't experience a single air attack. There was the one time when two small single-propeller planes flew overhead. Although they didn't drop any bombs a few shots were fired at them, since no one was sure whether they belonged to Biafra or Nigeria. Fortunately, neither one of them was hit. We soon learned that they were Minicoins, Biafran fighter planes, also fondly called *Biafran Babies*. (Minicoins is derived from Miniature Counterinsurgency.) A few of these charming planes were acquired towards the end of the war and Biafrans applauded their awesome and mythical capabilities, citing real or imagined instances where they inflicted enormous human and material damage on the enemy.

With the optimism introduced by the likes of the Minicoins, it was cause for much concern when, one night, the sounds of mortar fire came too close. They were loud and got louder and louder with each passing moment. Ukpong had since returned to his parents and my father was not at home. It was just my family and Goddy, my mother's faithful driver who had stayed with us throughout the war. There were also some of the military and civilian aides. We all panicked and some of the aides actually fled the house, abandoning us. The only available vehicle was Goddy's Peugeot 404 station wagon, which wasn't in the best shape. My mother quickly arranged for him to evacuate us from the camp and in minutes we packed the little we could into the boot and third row of seats and took off with as many people as the car could carry, which were my mother, Charles, me, Francis and Ime. None of the aides came along and neither did my father's mother and stepmother, or Mama Nkechi and her children. Later, my father saw to their safety.

Except for its ability to haul luggage, Goddy's trusted car served little purpose as it didn't move much faster than a toddler ambling down a rugged bush path. It was a dark night, and by the time we made it past the camp gate the roads were flooded with people fleeing the enemy incursion on foot. Like us, they didn't have a specific destination. Families, individuals, friends, couples, men, women and children all trudged along, carrying their miserable belongings in their hands and on their heads. Small children were strapped to their mothers' backs; otherwise, fathers or other older relatives carried them in their arms and on their shoulders. It was unusual, and something of a luxury, when a father managed to strap remnants of family belongings – or his children – on the back carriage and front crossbar of an old bicycle. He pushed and they moved slowly, but they made progress. The scenario was all too familiar.

Throughout the war Biafrans were constantly forced to move in a frantic search for safety and shelter. Whether on foot, by bicycle, or in vehicles that had been drained and stripped by overuse and poor maintenance, the people found a way to move each time the enemy came too close. One of the most poignant subplots that built around these movements was the agony that elderly men and women were subjected to. When a vehicle wasn't available they had to walk like everyone else. Aside from age, they had been depleted by hunger and the stress of the war. Often too weak there were, therefore, those who decided not to flee when everyone else, including family, sought to escape the enemy onslaught. They stayed back, submitting themselves to whatever fate the enemy brought. Some dared to walk and miraculously made it to a new location. Some dared to walk, but somewhere between where they started and an unknown destination collapsed or simply lay down and went to sleep. Not that it made a difference. Unable to drag the man or woman along, the people simply moved on, friends and relatives alike, perhaps weeping as they did so, perhaps offering their blessings.

Just as alarming was when there were too many children for fleeing parents and guardians to take along, or when one parent was saddled with the task. This wasn't uncommon since many Biafran homes were without men, and in some cases boys, as they were away fighting. When a fleeing mother faced the problem of being slowed down and apprehended by a ruthless enemy that rarely took prisoners, she often had to make the unbelievable choice of leaving behind a child, or children. The hope was that the enemy would be kinder to them than they had been to adults. Fortunately, Biafran soldiers always brought up the rear, gathering as many of the children as they could and eventually returning them to their families or delivering them to refugee camps. For those that were left behind, theirs was an uncertain fate that was either in the hands of an unpredictable enemy or the cold comfort of death.

Our car moved at about the same speed as the people; the only difference is that sometimes its exhaust let out a loud blast, a result of the miraculous Biafran fuel that it survived on. We continued at that slow pace until the Peugeot began to splutter and jerk repeatedly. Unfortunately this wasn't just a problem with the petrol. The spluttering and jerking continued and the car increasingly slowed until it came to a complete halt. Though it had put up a courageous struggle its engine had ceased altogether and no matter how hard Goddy tried he couldn't bring it back to life. We remained in that spot beside the road, speechless and clueless about what to do next, frightened by the fate that awaited us. Meanwhile, the fleeing crowds continued to stream by. We waited. It was the first time that we felt totally powerless and at the complete mercy of the war. In the past, and unlike most Biafrans, when we fled from the enemy we enjoyed the privilege of being transported in cars that were in good condition, and had access to some form of reasonable shelter. In this instance, we were as defenceless as the men, women and children who walked past us, barely noticing us. There were no physical or social barriers separating us now. Time passed and so did the people, in droves. I don't know how long we waited in terror until unexpected bright lights loomed in the distance. As the lights came closer it became obvious that a small convoy was heading our way. It finally arrived at where we were and slowed down, probably flagged down by Goddy. It was my father. His arrival brought a huge sense of relief that could only be likened to raising the dead. I suspect that he had come looking for us after reaching the house and discovering that we had fled. There was no time for pleasantries or formalities. He immediately arranged for us to be transferred to one of the vehicles in his small convoy. But convoy sizes were of no consequence at the time. I don't remember exactly where we were taken, but I remember a small house where we were received by a man. We spent the night there with no food, running water, or electricity, managing the little space as best as we could and sharing two or three available beds.

We left very early the next morning, transported in the same car and by the same driver that had brought us to our temporary refuge. I had no idea where we were going and didn't ask. The drive may have lasted about two hours, but what really stands out is an open lumbering lorry that we ended up driving behind for some of the journey. It was carrying bags of relief rice, some of which must have been torn as the grains trickled from the lorry down onto the road. People scrambled for the grains, scraping as much as they could off the road and putting them into enamel bowls, plastic bags, cups, all types of containers and their pockets, like they were storing gold. Even at my age, the pitiful sight, common as it was, caused something to well inside me. It was possibly the first time that I wondered if there would ever be an end to the madness.

It was still morning when we arrived at Nnewi, our head of state's hometown. Nnewi never fell to the enemy. When the war ended practically all of Biafra was overrun, except Nnewi. It appears that the young nation, in all its grief and depravation, had sworn that the hometown of its leader, its messiah, would remain sacred, untouched and intact. We were driven into a compound in which a large and elegant bungalow stood. On being guided into the house we met a rowdy spectacle and I immediately observed an opulence that I didn't know existed. There were several children in the house playing with an impressive array of toys, everything from cars and airplanes to trains and musical instruments. I was overwhelmed, perhaps intimidated, as must have been my older brother Charles. An adult offered us hot cups of chocolaty Bournvita which I had not seen or tasted since the war began almost three years earlier. I savoured the taste as it returned to me. The same adult encouraged us to play with some of the toys. We tried but were too estranged from this setting and its mystique and therefore couldn't enjoy playing there, not even if the toys were supremely enticing.

I soon understood that we were in Ojukwu's personal home. Two of the children were his while the rest were children of relatives. Except for the civilian and military servants, the adults in the house were also his relatives. In a short while we were ushered out of the house and spent the rest of the day under a shaded area within the compound where we were generally left alone. When we were not sitting on benches that had been provided, Charles and I played together to keep ourselves company. In the afternoon we were served *garri* and *egusi* (melon) soup, which was very welcome since it was the first real meal we had eaten since the previous afternoon.

Later that afternoon we were surprised and delighted when my father's official car drove into the compound. Its license plate still flaunted three metal stars while the flag mounted on its bonnet fluttered freely. It was not accompanied by a single vehicle, let alone a convoy, which was unusual and foreboding. Even more curious was that my father didn't come to see us throughout the time he spent in the compound. After conducting whatever business he had in the main house, he simply got into his car and was chauffeured out. Years later I learned that he had come to appeal to Ojukwu to allow my mother and us to be airlifted out of the country along with his family. Plans had apparently been concluded to fly the head of state's family and extended family out of the country before he would also leave 'in search of peace abroad'. My father was particularly eager for my mother to leave since she was pregnant with Philippa who would be born in the Ivory Coast in April 1970, three months from the time. Ojukwu granted my father's request.

I didn't realize how lucky we were until I heard, long after the war was over, that my aunt, Mama Nkechi, had pleaded with Ojukwu to allow at least one of her children to be taken on one of the frantic flights that were departing Biafra at this time. Her hope was that the child would preserve the family name for posterity if she and her other children didn't survive the final onslaught. The head of state refused her request; maybe he had no choice. The awkwardness of that incident is heightened by the fact that Mama Nkechi had known Ojukwu when they were much younger and her mother had been a close friend of Ojukwu's mother.

That evening we were transported out of His Excellency's compound. I had no idea that we were being taken to Uli Airport for the purpose of being flown out of Biafra. Uli Airport was the last surviving airfield through which Biafra transported or received people and shipments. I knew that we had arrived at an extremely important location because of the tight security in the area, which caused traffic to build up. All car lights were required to be switched off and the darkness was sinister, except for an occasional torchlight that indicated human movement. We were slowly directed forward along with other cars until we reached an open area where there was clearly an upsurge in activity. The lighting was still kept to a minimum as we stepped out of our vehicle carrying the few bags that we had with us.

I understood at this point that we were at some type of airport, albeit a small one, as a two-propeller cargo plane stood a few feet away from us. People were boarding the aircraft; it was a systematic and thorough process that stipulated privilege in the order of everything. Those responsible for ushering people onto the plane took their time, even though the entire atmosphere suggested urgency. As they announced family names, groups of people boarded by means of a ladder that was placed against the side of the craft. Although some were able to lug a bag or two when they climbed the ladder, for the most part pieces of luggage were tossed to passengers after they were on board. When Ojwuku's mother was invited to board the plane, climbing the ladder proved to be too strenuous for the old woman. A man had to stand under the ladder for her to use his head as an extra rung, which also served to reduce the space between the rungs. Other members of the general's larger family were on hand to board the plane. They formed a rather large crowd, which explains why they had all gathered at his home earlier in the day.

In a day or two, the head of state, accompanied by some of his top officials, would also leave the country, announcing a search for peace and a final solution to the Biafran tragedy. My father would take over as head of state – for a few days.

The plane carrying Ojukwu's family departed and finally my family was invited to board another plane, which we did with relative ease: my mother (despite her pregnancy), Charles, me, Ime and little Francis who would turn five the following month. With the help of attendants at the airstrip we hauled our bags onto the plane. That this was happening was intriguing, but that it was all happening so fast was beyond comprehension. After all, only the previous evening we still resided at Owerri. Because it was a cargo plane, it didn't have seats. We simply placed our belongings on the floor and sat on them. It wasn't long before the plane's engines came to life and through its windows we could see, in the dim light, the propellers gaining speed. It taxied down the single runway of the Uli Airport, built up speed and finally amassed enough strength to take off. Once we were airborne, Biafra began to fade and I knew it was the last time that I would set eyes on the young courageous nation whose ingenuity, confidence and willpower remains an example for history and humanity.

I knew that our departure had something to do with our safety, though I didn't know what the specific plans were. Ever since we moved out of AN Barracks it had become routine for us to relocate for the purpose of safeguarding ourselves. The difference in this instance is that our means of transportation was an airplane, an indication that we were going somewhere that was farther away. Because of the presence of my mother, with whom I always felt safe, I wasn't afraid. Like other passengers on the aircraft I was silent. I was also somber and not doing a lot of thinking, perhaps because I was too young to be conscious of a lot of things. It didn't occur to me that we shouldn't have been sitting on the floor of a plane in flight and that this plane, like others owned by Biafra, was maintained well below accepted standards. Chances are that it was in poor condition and wouldn't have been airborne except that the urgency of the situation left us with little choice. The flight could easily have been our last but staying back in Biafra didn't present a brighter picture.

Even though I didn't know it at the time, our destination was the beautiful Central African island-nation of São *Tomé*, one of the few countries that was sympathetic to the Biafran cause and misery. It was our first stop in a series of stops aimed at rediscovering ourselves. It was also here that we were issued the Biafran travel documents that would see us through our future destinations. Unlike standard passports, they only guaranteed exit from Biafra, no re-entry. In any case, there would be no Biafra to re-enter.

Chapter 9

The grass on which the elephants wrestled

Our flight from Biafra has prompted many fantastic stories: true, almost true, or outright false. One of them stayed with me: the claim that our plane was fired at by embittered Biafrans who couldn't understand why some of us were being transported to safety while they had to stay back to endure the consequences of a convoluted mess not of their making. Another version of the story claimed that it was actually Nigerian soldiers who shot at our plane as we flew over enemy-captured parts of a shrinking Biafra on our way to safety.

It is true that there was pandemonium, fear and rage as insufficient cargo planes airlifted fortunate Biafrans out of the country when it was on the brink of final collapse. There also had to be a measure of truth, at least to the several stories alleging that some of these planes were shot at by resentful Biafran soldiers as they sprinted down and took off from the Uli runway. Hysteria grew after Ojukwu boarded one of these flights on 9 January 1970 after broadcasting to the people that his mission was to secure permanent peace. His destination was the Ivory Coast, another sympathizer, where he was given asylum by then President Félix Houphouët-Boigny.

Though Biafra had a new head of state in my father, he didn't embody the mystique and invincibility that the people had associated with Ojukwu over the war years. With Ojukwu's sudden departure panic intensified, as did the scramble to leave Biafra, producing more fantastic stories that we were to hear in the coming months. Desperate Biafrans supposedly descended on Uli Airport in droves, alone and with their families, in attempts to board the now-treasured cargo planes. Standard procedures were gradually all but abandoned. My father, as the new Biafran head of state, was officially responsible for issuing authorization for exit. But he was largely bypassed as people went to Uli with the intension of forcing their way onto any available planes, regardless of the presence of soldiers who were supposed to maintain order. The soldiers – inadequate, poorly armed and more concerned about their own safety and that of their families – were increasingly incapable of controlling the angry, frantic crowds. Fights broke out as people struggled to board planes. People were injured, clothes were torn and ladders placed against the sides of aircraft were fractured from too many people trying to climb them at the same time. Sometimes a few family members who were able to get on board had to leave others behind who didn't make it. One rumour was that one of Biafra's top generals, Brigadier Effiong Udo Okon, managed to board one of the planes after engaging in a fierce struggle with other hopeful passengers, losing one of his shoes in the process. Distressingly, his wife and children, also at the airport, failed to board the plane with him. There was the story of the man who couldn't get on a plane; not giving up he started to chase after the aircraft as it taxied towards the runway. He was decapitated by a propeller.

Despite the possibility of inevitable embellishment, there was a lot of truth to these stories. Biafra was wrapped in terror, despair and anxiety, all of which were aggravated by Ojukwu's exit.

I don't know if our seatless plane was shot at, whether by Nigerian or Biafran soldiers or both. If that was the case, evidently a hit wasn't scored and we were therefore fortunate to arrive safely in São Tomé in the early hours of the morning.

When we got off the plane at São Tomé it was as if I was breathing fresh air for the first time, having just escaped the sweltering confinement of a fierce oven. The oven could have been the plane or all of Biafra. For the first time in three years I was without fear or doubt. I felt and smelled the calm all at once. It wasn't just the air and beauty of an airport that boasted a modern standard that Uli lacked completely; it was the deep-seated knowledge that I would no longer hear the sounds of gunshots or explosives, or cringe at the thought of an unannounced air raid. It was the awareness that I would see houses, trees, people and cars without worrying about the presence of corpses, shell-shocked soldiers, sickly elders, or malnourished children in their midst. It was the understanding that from then on if we changed homes it would be because we chose to do so and not because we were forced to abandon a dangerous location for the relative safety of another one.

The image of a new paradise was briefly disrupted as two airport workers, for whatever reason, got into a furious argument and then a fistfight not too far from where we had disembarked. They were quickly separated.

Shortly after we were escorted into the airport building, the name of the wife of the Secretary to the Biafran Government was announced: Mrs Margaret Akpan. She had been on the cargo plane with us along with her two daughters, Néné and Ekamma and her cousin Eme, who doubled as a nanny. They were eventually taken to and accommodated in a separate home from us. We were taken to the home of Mr Vin Muoneke, Biafra's Special Representative to São Tomé, where a number of other Biafran refugees were already staying. It was his wife who essentially hosted us since he was away during most of our stay there.

We spent about two weeks in São Tomé, which I remember to be a gorgeous island. Still a colony of Portugal it had a significant number of Europeans residing there and they were the main drivers of the luxury cars and motorcycles that crisscrossed the streets around us. Once in a while we heard the sounds of crabs being crushed by the speeding tyres. They emerged from the surrounding Atlantic Ocean and haplessly crawled onto the busy roads. We were occasionally taken on tours of the island where we took in its natural beauty more closely, including the recreational facilities that had been built mainly for its Portuguese and other European residents. These were not extended trips, they involved visits to restaurants and other places where privileged people went to unwind and while away the time. I think they may have been organized to free us from the monotony of spending all day at the Muoneke home. But they were a welcome breath of fresh air, literally, as movement in Biafra, whether long or short distance, was not without the threat of an air raid or the sight of a disoriented beggar, homeless drifter, or starving child. We remained in the car that chauffeured us around the island; viewed people, places and things through its windows; we never interacted with the local people. The outings may have lasted thirty to forty-five minutes, after which we were taken back to our temporary home.

Because our escape had been abrupt with scant planning, things happened spontaneously and we soon understood that there was little rationale to where we had been taken or what happened to us. With limited communication systems at the time there couldn't have been any elaborate exchange of ideas on what to do with Biafran refugees in different locations abroad. Despite its collapse, however, Biafra still had international envoys who continued to play diplomatic roles, especially in countries like São Tomé, Portugal, France, the Ivory Coast and Gabon, which had recognized, or at least sympathized, with Biafra. Working with their foreign counterparts, these envoys prepared our itineraries, ensured that our papers were up-to-date, and provided much-needed cash for our basic survival.

We were not surprised, therefore, when we were chauffeured from the Muoneke home back to São Tomé's airport to continue our voyage out of Biafra. Our next stop was Lisbon, Portugal. At the airport we reconnected with Mrs Akpan and her family who apparently were also bound for Lisbon; we would travel together. Unlike the one that flew us out of Biafra, the plane scheduled to take us to Lisbon was a much larger four-propeller plane. Both planes had something in common, they were seatless cargo planes that made our rescue from Biafra possible. Whatever my reservations were, I was now at least no longer scared. We boarded the large plane, placed our modest luggage on the floor and sat on it. There was ample space on the plane since our two families were the only passengers, except for a middle-aged white man who sat in a corner by himself. I slept through most of the very long flight.

Even if administrative decisions were haphazard and on the spur of the moment, we were managed quite efficiently. In Portugal we were lodged in the Hotel Infante Santo where my mother and Mrs Akpan shared a room. Charles, Frances, Ime, and I shared another room along with Mrs Akpan's daughters and Eme.

I was captivated by the luxury of the hotel, especially since it was a massive departure from the deprivation we had left behind in Biafra. For two weeks we stayed there, occasionally taking walks in the city but never venturing too far from the hotel. We were refugees, not vacationers, and didn't have access to any form of transport. Our walks were intended to break the boredom of spending all day in a hotel room, and because Mrs Akpan and my mother didn't accompany us we were supervised by Ime and Eme. The busyness of Lisbon reminded me of Lagos, except that its traffic jams were heavier, its buildings were taller, and its weather was much colder.

We looked forward to breakfast as we were always served tall glasses of cold chocolate milk with our meals, for which we never failed to say, *obrigado*. Sometimes we went down to the lobby and watched shows on a small black-and-white television, even though we didn't understand what was being said. It was the first time we were watching television since the early stages of the war.

Apart from our walks, the only other time we left the hotel was when we were chauffeured to a house where a number of ex-Biafrans were gathered. They must have been escapees like us, though we had evidently departed Biafra on different dates and on different cargo planes. My mother and the other adults spoke freely with one another, which made sense since they were most likely from prominent Biafran families and knew each other before their arrival in Lisbon. As was usual in spaces dominated by adults, we, the children, mostly watched, talked to our siblings or friends if we had any, or kept our thoughts to ourselves. The house may have been the residence of a Biafran diplomat, though I am not sure, just like I am not sure why we were taken there. Perhaps it was to notify us of plans for our future travels and safety. Or it may have just been a get-together and an opportunity to feed us Nigerian food, since we were all eventually served rice and stew before we returned to our different temporary lodgings. As with other experiences since leaving Biafra, this one only stirred my curiosity; it provided no concrete answers to our situation. It didn't frighten me but contributed to the vagueness of all that was happening around us.

We were finally airlifted out of Portugal, leaving Mrs Akpan and her family behind. I don't know how long they remained there or where they were eventually taken; my parents re-established contact with the Akpan family after we returned to Nigeria several months later. Charles and I would not see Ekamma and Néné until we all attended the University of Calabar, in Nigeria, between the late 1970s and early 1980s, though only at overlapping times. Mrs Akpan, a distinguished teacher, went on to establish Aunty Margaret International School, a primary school to which a secondary school was later added. It remains one of the premier institutions in Calabar. I am still in touch with Ekamma who now runs her late mother's school.

In the end, there was no real purpose to our flight and stay in Portugal, though we enjoyed our time at the hotel. It may have all been a logistical blunder since our final destination, I later discovered, was supposed to be the Ivory Coast, which is a relatively short flight from São Tomé. Instead we had travelled a few thousand miles in the wrong direction.

But we didn't fly straight to the Ivory Coast from Portugal. We actually went further north first, stopping in Geneva and then Paris. Because I didn't know we were supposed to be going to the Ivory Coast and that our extended flight was unnecessary, none of this bothered me. In Paris we exited the airport as my mother needed to buy clothes for us, but more importantly, new shoes for Ime. The search was filled with drama as no female shoes could be found that were large enough to house Ime's enormous feet. After visiting several shoe stores my frustrated mother had to settle for the only solution, which was to buy unisex boots for her. Looking back, I imagine my mother, who was about six months pregnant, must have been incredibly frustrated and encumbered by what seemed like an unending and indefinite crisscrossing of countries. I was still too young to appreciate the difficulties that come with bearing a child.

It was also in Paris, either during the drive out of or to the airport, that I noticed a large billboard displaying a picture of a starving Biafran child. Even though we had covered thousands of miles in an effort to discard the trauma of the war, the picture seemed to predict that we would be eternally haunted by its grisly images.

We finally made the long flight from Paris to Abidjan, then capital of the Ivory Coast. Thankfully, after leaving Lisbon, we would no longer fly in cargo planes. The comfort of real seats was very welcome. In Abidjan we were lodged in a modest hotel for a few days where we all shared a large room with beds partitioned by curtains. But Abidjan was not our final destination; it was Bouaké, five hours north of Abidjan near the middle of the country.

On the day that we left Abidjan we were provided with a car

and driver. The drive was long and tiring. In the few days after we arrived at Bouaké we were visited and welcomed by the mayor and his sister and introduced to former Biafran families that had arrived before us. Bouaké had become the de facto West African city of refuge for fugitive Biafrans. Ojukwu's many relatives occupied a bungalow not too far from the one in which we were now housed.

The house that stood beside ours was occupied by Mr Douglas Ngube, a former Biafran official, his wife, son and daughter. Major General Alexander Madiebo, Biafra's one-time Army Commander, lived further away from us with his wife and children. Ojukwu, his wife, son, daughter and some Biafran officers were given accommodation in Yamoussoukro, the hometown of President Houphouët-Boigny.

It didn't take long for us to start interacting with the small ex-Biafran community in Bouaké, visiting each other quite frequently. In the end, however, most of the friends that Charles and I made didn't come from the world of refugees. Next door to us was a large yard containing small homes that were either being rented or that may have belonged to an extended family. Charles and I made friends with children in the yard and occasionally went there to play with them. I remember Lukman and Ladje. Lukman was close in age to us while Ladje must have been a teenager and therefore significantly older. We were impressed by the fact that Ladje could speak English, which removed the language barriers that sometimes existed between us and people in the area.

We explored Bouaké and built new friendships with boys in the neighbourhood with whom we played football and a game in which we used marbles to aim at and hit other marbles with our thumbs. The more our friendships grew, the more we learned French words and phrases. Wherever we encountered the people of Bouaké – whether we walked through neighbourhoods, bought bonbon glacé (ice candy) from vendors, or played with children in our neighbourhood – they were kind and courteous. They were welcoming, genuinely wanting to know who we were, and were patient in dealing with our limited knowledge of French. It is possible that they had been notified about the arrival of Biafrans to their community. If that were the case it makes sense that they were intentionally warm towards us. But it is equally likely that they were a warm and hospitable people anyway. Their government had been sympathetic to the Biafran struggle and widely represented Biafrans as victims of ethnic-centred genocidal attacks.

But our world was to expand in other ways.

Among Ojukwu's relatives was a young girl named Nkali, who might have been slightly older than Charles and me. She was eventually taken to Ireland, perhaps with some of her other relatives. When some months later Charles and I also relocated to Ireland; we were surprised and amused when Valentine told us about the day he had met a fair-skinned girl named Nkali who was related to Ojukwu. It happened at a gathering organized at a club that periodically entertained children from overseas. Valentine was clearly enamoured with Nkali's beauty as he kept asking her to dance with him.

In 2014 when we lived in Accra, Ghana, I was approached at a friend's reception by a tall woman who asked if I was Philip Effiong. Surprised, I said, 'Yes I am'. She went on to explain that she had known me and my brothers in 1970 when we all lived in Bouaké and went to school at a refugee camp.

'You haven't changed since then', she said.

I was just as perplexed at her recollection as I was flattered by the thought of having preserved my youthful looks all those years. I asked her who she was.

'I am Nkali,' she responded.

My jaw dropped.

'And this is my daughter.'

She pointed to a teenage girl who looked just like her. I smiled and nodded at the girl who smiled in return. We chatted about our time at Bouaké without necessarily going into any details. We also talked about how and why we ended up in Accra at the time, our careers and what had happened to our families over the years. As if rehearsed, we avoided any reference to Biafra or her uncle, Biafra's erstwhile commander-in-chief. At the end of the reception Nkali left with her daughter, while we returned to our home at the AU Village.

Though I have run into many people that were a part of my Biafran world and story, no encounter has been as unexpected and as intriguing as that one. It was a reminder that the dispersal of families from Biafra had created many other dispersals and intriguing plots and subplots. In the process we had grown and transformed in diverse social, cultural, educational and professional ways. My continued hope is that none of the plots or subplots ended tragically.

Beyond our neighbourhood, we were occasionally given rides into the city, mainly to shop for provisions at Monoprix, a supermarket. A driver was assigned to us for that purpose; I remember him to be quite the gentleman. He was large and bubbly, always dressed professionally, treated my mother with the utmost respect and performed his job diligently. One day, as he drove us home, perhaps from a trip to food stores, he decided to stop by at his home and introduce us to his wife and child. The home was modest and decent and the driver came across as a doting husband and devoted father.

Apart from occasional visits from the mayor, we were one day invited to his imposing residence where we were served snacks and drinks. I remember that he had a large tiger, which, on entry to the property, could be seen chained to an area near the gate. It was the first time that I had seen a tiger up close.

On another day we were chauffeured from Bouaké to Yamoussoukro, about a two-hour drive. We were to visit Ojukwu. He was housed in a splendid bungalow, which we later learned was one of several private homes owned by the Ivorian president along a beautiful stretch of road. We also learned that Biafran officers who had left with Ojukwu occupied another bungalow on the same stretch of road. Across the road was a splendid lake, allegedly home to a large community of crocodiles, though we didn't see any that day.

This was our first meeting with Ojukwu since our chance encounter with him on our way to (or was it from?) Owerri during the final stages of the war. Because I knew he was no longer head of state he didn't command the aura of omnipotence that I once associated with him. It was also the first time I was seeing him in civilian clothing, which looked commonplace and didn't generate the military might I associated with his spruce army uniforms, bedecked with glitzy insignias. Somehow I understood this and wasn't disappointed that his magnificence had waned. We were, after all, in the Ivory Coast and not in Biafra where he had been perceived as a masterful military strategist and a somewhat Christ-like figure. He was now husband and father and the proof was in the presence of his wife, the elegant Aunty Njideka, his son Emeka Jr, and his daughter Mimi. Even at my age I could see the striking resemblance that Emeka Jr had to his father, though the latter flaunted a generous clump of facial hair that his young son wouldn't inherit until many years later. Ojukwu's affection for his daughter was unmistakable as he kept calling out to her, lifting her onto his knees and teasing her fondly. My mother spent most of the time speaking with Ojukwu and Aunty Njideka, while Charles, Francis and I sat in a section of the living room, not interested in their conversation. Because we were unfamiliar with the house and its surroundings we hardly moved and didn't venture outside at all. If the Ojukwu children hadn't been so young they might have led us out to play. Lunch came as a welcome relief because of our long, tiring trip earlier in the day. We were served rice and stew by domestic servants that had been assigned to Ojukwu. After lunch we returned to Bouaké before it got dark.

The most significant excursions outside our neighbourhood were when we began to attend classes at a refugee camp for children who had been rescued from Biafra when the war was still raging. The camp Nkali had referred to. It flaunted male and female dormitories, a cafeteria, playing fields and a row of classrooms. Age may have been the determinant for class placement rather than academic level.

Not long after we settled in Bouaké, Charles, Francis and I were enrolled at the school. Because they had arrived ahead of us, Madiebo's children and young members of Ojukwu's extended family were taking lessons there long before us. Children who stayed at the camp could easily be distinguished from those of us who came from outside because they dressed in brown khaki uniforms. Ranging in age from toddler to teenager, it was evident that the refugees were being well taken care of, even if they had been sick and starving on arrival. They were vibrant and cheerful and during breaks wasted no time to swarm the fields where they played football and other games. We gladly joined them and made new friends. One of them was especially close to Charles and me. I believe his name was Godwin and remember him as soft-spoken and full of stories about the camp. We admired his football skills and sometimes watched him as he demonstrated his dribbling magic on the field. Our interactions with these friends only took place when we were at the camp. On weekends and after school we didn't spend time with them. Under different circumstances we could have forged stronger and more lasting ties.

When I recall the anguish, deprivation and deaths at refugee camps in Ifakala, I realize how fortunate the refugees at Bouaké were. If they had remained in Biafra most of them would have died or been permanently maimed by any of several mental or physical ailments. Today many of those refugees are business owners and professionals in various parts of the world and have gone on to raise children and grandchildren of their own. They were not only given renewed hope in Bouaké but became the protagonists of success stories that would have eluded them if they hadn't been delivered from the massive and erratic onslaught that Biafra endured. The leadership and people of the Ivory Coast at the time are therefore deserving of much gratitude, as are the numerous organizations and individuals who, in various self-sacrificial and risky ways, embarked on projects that guaranteed safety and rebirth for defenceless Biafran children in the Ivory Coast and other parts of the world, even in Biafra.

After the war, the refugees were systematically returned to Nigeria where they were reunited with parents, other family members, or family friends. Some of them were never taken back because their kin couldn't be located. They remained in the Ivory Coast and have gone on to create a community of descendants of former Biafran refugees, which has increasingly integrated with Ivorian communities over the years.

Education at the refugee camp, though improvised in many ways, was a welcome departure from the fairly predictable life that we lived in our neighbourhood. We started the day with an assembly and prayers before marching in organized formation to our various classes. Different teachers, some of whom had accompanied the refugees from Biafra, visited our classes and taught us basic subjects like maths, English and science. One of the teachers stood out because of his unfailing sense of humour and endless supply of jokes. He was a Catholic priest, most likely from Ireland. Break time was always anticipated as we looked forward to being served slices of cake.

One of the highlights of our time at the refugee camp was when the students put together a theatrical performance. We observed their colourful rehearsals after regular class times, which sometimes caused us to stay at the camp long after school closed for the day. In the end, the show was a spectacular meeting of various art forms, including music, dance, song, poetry and drama. The creativity and talent exhibited by the refugees was exceptional, all of which would have been lost forever if fate hadn't removed them from Biafra.

Bouaké was kind in many other ways too. Except for language, the people were very much like us in lifestyle, clothing and foods. We were at home and even the language gap was gradually narrowed as we learned more French words and expressions. When things got a little complicated, like when my mother needed to give elaborate instructions to our night watchman, she solicited the help of interpreters. They were mainly Igbo teachers at the camp who were fairly well-versed in French.

My mother started to receive several visits from Mrs Regina Madiebo, sometimes at night. I didn't understand at the time that she was a nurse and was carefully monitoring my mother who was in her final month of pregnancy and close to going into labour. Despite my naiveté I understood that my mother was going to have a baby when our driver chauffeured her to the hospital and returned without her. For the next few days we remained under the care of Ime. And then the news was delivered, I believe by one of the ladies in the Ojukwu household.

'Your mummy has given birth. It's a girl.'

We had all hoped for a baby girl, especially my mother who already had four sons and had lost a daughter in childbirth. The news was a profound reason to be happy, something that had become increasingly rare in Biafra. In a day or two Charles, Francis and I were taken to the hospital to see the baby. We were thrilled by how precious she looked, which swelled the happiness we felt. A bowl filled with grapes sat on the table next to my mother's bed. She invited us to eat them. We didn't need any persuasion. It was the first time in my life that I tasted grapes. They remain one of my favourite fruits and an associative link to my little sister.

Somehow my parents continued to exchange letters, thanks to the efforts of Biafran envoys abroad and foreign sympathizers, some of whom may have been secretly active within Nigeria. This was quite a feat since the Nigeria that my father resided in was still in the early post-war phase of uncertainty, rebuilding and a great deal of fragility. A few weeks after my mother gave birth my father received the news. Despite the victimization he faced, his joy was evident in the response he sent her, which she read to us. He named the baby Philippa, making her his second namesake after me. Prior to the arrival of my father's letter, the baby had not been formally named, though the mayor's sister had casually named her after herself – Mary Therese. A few weeks later Philippa was baptized. The ceremony was performed by our Catholic priest-teacher in a classroom that doubled as a chapel. Ojukwu's mother served as godmother.

But just as the letters between my parents celebrated life, they also lamented loss. One afternoon I walked into our kitchen to discover Ime leaning against a wall sobbing. I immediately went and reported what I had seen to my mother who explained that news had just been received of some of our relatives who had died during the war. Though we had lost contact with them we were unaware of their deaths. They included Ime's youngest brother (Asuquo), her stepmother (Eka Comfort), my grandfather (Ekamba Ete) and my father's personal cook (Eyo Bassey Inyang).

Other news reached us too, including confirmation that Biafra no longer existed. Its demise became official after my father led a delegation to Lagos to broker a peace deal with the Nigerian government and declared loyalty to the federal military government. For my mother the news was both reassuring and troubling, especially after she learned that my father had been arrested and detained. Before she returned to Nigeria in the coming months to be reunited with him, she lived in fear and desperation, tormented by the overwhelming possibility that she might never see him again.

We accepted Bouaké as our new home and were adjusting well. But it was also to be a temporary home. About two months after Philippa was born my mother informed Charles and me that we would be moving to Ireland too. The purpose was to reintroduce us to conventional schooling without necessarily scoffing at the haphazard and makeshift education that Biafra and Bouaké had served us. We would join our elder brother and sisters – Valentine, Rosalyn and Mercy – who were among the young Biafrans that had been taken to Ireland long before the war ended. We received the news with mixed feelings. On the one hand we were excited about going to Ireland, not necessarily because of the promise of improved education, but because we missed our brother and sisters. On the other hand, however, we didn't want to be separated from our newborn sister whom everyone had grown so fond of.

Close to the date of our trip, my mother repeatedly drilled into our heads the travel instructions that we had to memorize and observe strictly for our flight from Abidjan to Dublin. Only then did we realize that we were to be unaccompanied. Charles was only eleven while I was nine. A few days before our flight my mother, with baby Philippa, Francis and Ime, accompanied Charles and I to Abidjan where we stayed in a guesthouse. The highlight of our brief stay was when we were invited to the home of Professor Kenneth Dike for dinner. One of Biafra's roving ambassadors, Dike was also one of Africa's finest historians.

The day of our flight finally arrived and we all went to the airport where Charles and I said our final goodbyes to our family. Because our mother had repeatedly emphasized the instructions we were to follow, we believed that we knew what to do. My confidence was heavily dependent on Charles's, which was unshakeable.

The flight from Abidjan to Dublin was smooth and without incident, except for the time when I wept hysterically because a layover lasted much longer than we expected.

At Dublin Airport, before Charles and I were introduced to our host family, the O'Connells, we met and hugged Valentine, Rosalyn and Mercy who had been brought to the airport by their host family, the Murphys. Our conversation was predictable.

'How was your flight?'

'It was okay.'

'How is mummy and Francis and the baby?'

'They are well.'

'It's been such a long time. It's so good to see you again.'

'It is good to see you.'

We also greeted Mr and Mrs Murphy who welcomed us to Ireland. We might have said more and expressed greater excitement if we weren't so tired from our trip. Besides, we were overwhelmed by the strange world that we found ourselves in, one filled with unfamiliar faces. To compound things, we were without the shield that I always relied on in times of uncertainty – my parents, especially my mother.

Everyone then accompanied us to the O'Connell home at Hyde Park Gardens in Blackrock, where Charles and I were accommodated and nurtured for the next seven months. Although the O'Connells had four sons, the two oldest, Michael and Jim, had left the house and were training to be priests while the other two, Brendan and Declan, were still at home. Brendan attended Blackrock College in Dublin, which is also where Valentine went to school. Rosalyn and Mercy attended Dominican Convent in Cabra, near Dublin.

Life at the O'Connell home was comfortable; they were gracious and generous. We ate three good meals each day and had a bedroom to ourselves. Charles and I were introduced to the table tennis table located in one of the ground-floor rooms; we were immediately enthralled. We learned fast and spent extended periods almost every day competing against ourselves or against Declan and Brendan. At the back of the house was a small field and a garden in which an apple tree grew. When the fruit ripened, we gladly plucked and ate them. It was also on the backyard field that the O'Connell brothers and their friends taught us how to play cricket. On Sundays we unfailingly attended church. There were also weekdays when we attended church for any of several reasons.

It didn't take long before Charles and I made friends with other children in Hyde Park Gardens. I don't recall any prejudices as they all embraced us sincerely and happily. Our games revolved around football on the quiet streets, cowboy battles, or hide and seek. One outdoor activity didn't involve playing with other children, though children were central to it. It was Halloween on 31 October, the only Halloween I ever participated in. I was dressed as a gorilla and after a debate over the need for me to either wear or not wear gloves, it was agreed that I didn't need them since my palms were brown enough. On that day, Charles and I received a lot of sweets and unshelled peanuts.

Long before Halloween the O'Connell's took the entire family on a summer vacation that revealed the vast beauty of Ireland beyond what we had come to know. We were taken to the gorgeous Aran Islands, first stopping at the majestic harbour city of Galway where we spent a few days with friends of the O'Connells. At the Aran Islands, we stayed in a hotel resort for about two weeks. One of the halls in the hotel had a table tennis table which Charles and I periodically used to sharpen our skills. Otherwise, we toured the islands and spent a significant amount of time at the beach. We also visited breath-taking sites like cliffs overhanging parts of the Atlantic Ocean and caves that had allegedly been the homes of monks. With its dirt roads, thatched houses and horse-driven carts, the Aran Islands reminded me of rural communities in Biafra and Nigeria.

Considering the amount of money that the O'Connells spent on our vacation, which was a drastic departure from the ugliness of the war, I could not thank them enough. I was delighted to reconnect with Declan forty-seven years later and continue to stay in touch with him.

But even in the midst of what seemed like a steady settling down to a new routine and lifestyle, we couldn't completely escape the Biafran scourge, which continued to linger in various shapes. Whenever a plane flew overhead, though not often, I cringed, afraid that it would drop rockets and bombs on us. On this particular day, the plane may have been exceptionally loud or low, I don't recall. But I panicked and ran to the back of the house where I hid under a tree. No one seemed to notice that I was not in the house, which wasn't unusual since I was frequently out on the streets playing with other children in the neighborhood. I was also worried for Mrs O'Connell who had stepped out, perhaps to the grocery store. If the plane dropped bombs or fired rockets, she could be hit and injured or, even worse, killed. I was therefore very relieved when she returned home safe and sound and found me hiding under the tree. She asked me what I was doing there and I explained my anxieties regarding the plane that had flown by about an hour earlier.

Charles and I were eventually enrolled in Class Six and Four at St. Mary's Boys' National School in Booterstown. After breakfast on weekdays we walked to the school, which wasn't a problem though it was quite a distance away. We learned the direction from one of the older O'Connell boys who first took us there. On our way to and from school Charles and I took in the landscape and geography of that section of Dublin, even playing games along the road. I am not sure how it was determined what classes we should be in since we had lost three to four years of a stable primary school education during the war. But we ended up performing quite well and were not intimidated by the academic work that we had to cope with. The school had a diverse group of students from various parts of the world, which helped Charles and me settle in easily and feel at home. Charles went on to play Gaelic Football for the school; it was a sport that we knew nothing about prior to coming to Ireland. He soon established himself as one of the school's sports stars.

There were some challenges in Ireland. We had been without haircuts in many months and our hair had become notoriously long and bushy. Mrs O'Connell did her best to manage our heads and would sit us down and pick through our hair with a comb. Charles's curly hair was easy to detangle but mine, the 'nappiest' in the family, was a different story. It took much longer for Mrs O'Connell to pick my tight knots and it always hurt tremendously, causing my eyes to water. One day Mrs

O'Connell decided to send us to a barber. The barber did his best but ultimately gave us bad haircuts.

Another problem was that Charles and I missed our parents whom we had never been away from for an extensive period. We had always had the company of at least one of them. The next best option would have been the company of our elder sisters and brother. However, they lived with the Murphys in another, not nearby, part of Dublin. We visited them occasionally, sometimes spending up to a weekend there. Mr Murphy, an architect, had once lived in Nigeria and contributed to the design of the Catholic Cathedral in the city of Owerri. He spoke pidgin English fluently and I seized every opportunity to speak with him, entertained by the fact that a white man could speak the language. The Murphys were exceedingly kind to Rosalyn, Mercy and Valentine.

Whenever it was time for me and Charles to return to the O'Connell home after visiting the Murphys, we cried. But this had nothing to do with the O'Connells or the Murphys; it was our way of lamenting the absence of our parents. It therefore came as good news when the O'Connell's intimated that we might soon be returning to Nigeria.

Chapter 10

The Biafran scar

Until our arrival in Dublin we had always identified as Biafrans. Our next international trip, about seven months after we arrived in Ireland, would take Charles and me back to Nigeria, at which time we had to discard our Biafran identities. Valentine, Rosalyn and Mercy were not to return with us; they returned several months later. I suspect it was because they had been in Ireland much longer than we had and were therefore being given the opportunity to complete their different school years. At the time I didn't care; I was simply happy to return to my parents, whether it was in Biafra or Nigeria. The O'Connell home had been a splendid bookend to the catastrophe that had befallen us and our country, and went a long way to closing our formal Biafran chapter.

After Charles and I resettled in Nigeria we found that our departure from Biafra was not actually complete. We were thrust into a twilight zone somewhere between Nigeria and Biafra. It gradually transformed into a ritual space on which we rehearsed our inevitable rites of passage from Biafran loyalists to Nigerian citizens. Of all our travels, therefore, this psychological journey would prove to be most challenging and vital. This is because so many unpredictable changes and uncertainties awaited us in Nigeria, including the fact that our parents had virtually lost all that they once owned and for which they had worked so hard. With the total destruction of our family home at Ikot Ekpene, we arrived at a situation of homelessness and near-destitution. Having been dismissed from the army without any benefits, we reunited with a father who was doomed to an endless and unstable life of struggle for day-to-day survival. If he had been a lawyer, teacher, or engineer in the army, he might have fallen back on any of these professions. But he had been a professional soldier and nothing else and therefore had nothing but the mercy of haphazard business transactions to turn to. In a society where he was widely branded and hated as the miscreant who tried to destroy Nigeria's sacred unity, this source of restoration would prove to be bitterly arduous and insufferable for him.

My mother shared in this burden of grappling with anxieties triggered by the lack of a steady livelihood. Though she had a teaching certificate that qualified her to teach at primary school level, she rarely played the role of schoolteacher; before the war she had mostly functioned as a homemaker and businesswoman. More than my father, therefore, she was more primed for a life of tracking business opportunities. Because I had never seen her design or sew clothes before the war, I was surprised when she set up a small sewing business, which proved to be invaluable among the other business ventures she explored after the war. I later learned that she had studied Art Design and Fashion at the Farnborough College of Technology when she accompanied my father to the United Kingdom during one of his several officer training courses.

We, the children, carried some of the weight too, though in a different and mostly psychological way. We were, after all, the children of Biafra's number-two man, the criminal rebel who tried to shatter Nigeria's unity and in the process betrayed his own Ibibio identity by conspiring with stubborn and self-absorbed Igbos who were at the forefront of the mad scheme. The coward who surrendered because he lacked the fearlessness of an authentic army general. To this day this stigma is still periodically thrown at us

Ours became an unrecognizable life that was widely defined by a combination of fear, success, failure, hope and despair. Thanks to the resilience and resolve of our parents, we had to find a way to cope with our circumstance and we did.

Evidently, therefore, when Charles and I embarked on a flight back to Nigeria along with about twenty other ex-Biafran children that had been granted refuge in Ireland, we were riding heavily on uncertainty. We didn't anticipate the turmoil that awaited us, which was really a continuation of the family disintegration that had begun when our quest for post-Biafra security landed us in different locations. Because our frantic efforts at restoration lacked certainty, they ended up being experiments at best. They were much like our shuffle across continents, which weren't always preceded by concrete plans or knowledge of specific destinations. But, as with those trips, some form of social and economic mobility had to be maintained after we all reassembled in a new Nigeria, otherwise dormancy would have set in and so would confusion and anguish.

Though our limbo was much like the clichéd cyclical trip devoid of purpose or conclusion, it promised an end because it had a beginning (the war) that was still visible and tangible. Our groping would finally become as mental as it was physical, as puzzling as it was regional. It became a prime shaper of our collective mind and soul, our collective willpower. It carved out a new world steeped in illusion and suspicion. It created a new narrative.

For us, therefore, another conflict had just begun.

Epilogue

War lives on in its aftermath and until such aftermath is completely eliminated (which is often unlikely), war rages on. For Biafra, this was despite the idealistic declaration of 'No Victor, No Vanquished'. Biafra lost the war; we were vanquished. This hard fact has been evident and is still evident in a number of ways that are sometimes veiled and at other times more obvious.

Oji River in present Enugu State has been the dismal home to destitute Biafran veterans, abandoned there since the war ended, left to wallow in the anguish of their mental and physical traumas. Though many of them have died, a large number still occupy this desolate world as virtual outcasts – sick, feeble, poor and largely invisible – and can be spotted on the Enugu–Onitsha highway in their wheelchairs begging for alms. It seems like the vindictiveness of their enemy is contagious, since their own brethren have also chosen to ignore them.

The 'abandoned property' scandal continues to deprive people of their homes and businesses fifty plus years after the war's end. It is a ruthless and insolent policy that blatantly tells the victim: *You abandoned your home and business during the war and therefore do not have any claim to it. As far as we are concerned, you no longer exist.*

Faith-based groups and individuals that delivered food, clothing, and medication to Biafra were not spared. The foreigners among them were particularly targeted and unceremoniously deported to wherever they had come from.

In 1972 my state, then South Eastern, refused to award me a secondary school scholarship that I had earned. My crime was that I am my father's son and easy to identify; after all, I bear his first and last name. In the eyes of the state, at least back then, he was the traitor son of the land who had conspired with Igbos to massacre his own people.

Until his death in November of 2003, I observed as my father struggled inconsolably and to no avail to recover from the collapse of his twenty-five-year military career, courtesy of events surrounding the war. His rejection by Nigeria was perhaps best expressed when in 1979 he wasn't allowed to contest for the office of Governor of Cross River State under the banner of the People's Redemption Party (PRP). Never holding a stable or fulltime job after Biafra ceased to exist, he (along with my mother) fabricated a means of livelihood for themselves, their family, and others with whom he had become acquainted by circumstance. Somehow, he invented a reason to prevail until he succumbed to the one phenomenon that always prevails – death. He must have known that his relentless demands for withheld benefits and entitlements were as annoying as they were futile, but he carried the demands to his grave.

Before this becomes the archetypal victim's whimper, let me make it clear that I have nothing to whimper about. The damage done to my father's mind and career notwithstanding, he still managed to feed, clothe, house and educate all his children. And despite that grating denial of a scholarship by my state, my education didn't suffer.

Naturally, my father gained some die-hard accusers and sworn enemies, but a significant number of them are dead; many actually died before him. Not one of them received anything compared to the national and international recognition and adulation that he received in death, a gratifying indication that the truth does indeed set one free. Resultantly I am not concerned by fabrications about the war or myths surrounding my father's role. The truth is bound to persist, along with its own brand of justice.

The Nigeria–Biafra War lives on in several scenarios. Ethnic sentiments have intensified; the military is yet to regain its former glory; there is still pervasive indignation and grief (perhaps mostly suppressed); the campaign for overdue benefits continues; the abandoned property drama is just one out of several persecutions resulting from the conflict. The war normalized violence as an acceptable means of achieving desires and various unfolding incidents read like a collection of grisly details in a horror movie.

- The fanatical Islamist movement, led by Mohammed Marwa (Maitatsine), shortly after the war in the 1970s, carried out killings in northern Nigeria, allegedly to halt the culture of material greed.
- Demolition of the family–business commune of legendary non-conformist musician Fela Anikulapo-Kuti, including physical assaults on its residents in 1977 by 'unknown soldiers'.
- The 1986 obliteration of outspoken journalist Dele Giwa by a parcel bomb.
- Wanton destruction of life and property by so-called Fulani herdsmen, mainly in the Middle Belt since the late 1990s.
- The battery, murder and banishment of hundreds of children from homes and communities since the early 2000s, thanks to their stigmatization as witches by nefarious Pentecostal pastors.
- Ruthless offensives executed by Boko Haram in its fantasy

quest to create a pure Islamist state in Nigeria since 2010.
- The massacre by the army of minority Shia Muslims in 2015, a group advocating for the creation of an Iranian-style state in Nigeria.
- The characteristic use of teargas, batons and live ammunition against peaceful demonstrators by law enforcement (including the army) often resulting in injury and death.
- Military attacks against civilian activists seeking security and self-determination in movements like EndSARS and pro-Biafra crusades.
- The notorious brutality of the Special Anti-Robbery Squad (SARS) since the 1990s.

These are just some examples; there are many more.

I am not at all shocked, or even surprised, by the current spate of violence that is increasingly enveloping Nigeria. This is just a consequence of the culture of sadism that many of us have embraced when it has been convenient for us to do so. We don't complain about present-day violence because we abhor violence; we complain because violence has finally come to our communities and doorsteps. This is something we should have foreseen, but failed to, when we tolerated violence because it happened far away and seemed to elude us. But it was a matter of time. Those who endorse the barbarity of the so-called civil war as a legitimate means to achieving unity are acting like the fool who sets his house on fire and then retires to one of the rooms to take a nap. It is a matter of time before he is consumed by the flames. I have never posed as a prophet, let alone a prophet of doom, but I dare say that we are currently, and increasingly being engulfed by the fire that we set to our home. If, therefore, Nigeria refuses to take stock of its history of sanctioned violence, which would entail speaking the truth, redressing its brutalities, apologizing and creating space for restitution, it will continue to spiral down a bottomless pit filled with rage, hatred, terror, blood, death, destruction and desolation. If Nigeria remains inattentive and indifferent to the generational and transgenerational consequences of its most vicious and vindictive mission – its unrestrained assault on Biafra – it will only continue to decline to a dysfunctional state where aggression in every assorted form becomes the favoured tool for economic and political success. As stated, I don't speak with the certainty of a prophet of doom, but with the conviction that only the truth will set us free.

Appendix

Index of Biafran War Songs

While some of these songs were created within the oral tradition, others were adaptations of Christian and other popular songs, which were revised to address themes of war. The Nigeria–Biafra War awakened the oral poet's creative impulse.

Songs rendered in English

For forty days and forty nights
I've been suffering for Gowon's sake
If I die, I don't care
'Cause Gowon must surely die

My darling I'm moving tonight, tonight
My darling I'm moving far away, far away
If I happen to die in the battlefield
Never mind, we shall meet again

My father, don't you worry
My mother, don't you worry
If I happen to die in the battlefield
Never mind, we shall meet again

If you want to collect your people
O Lord, O Lord
If you want to collect your people

Remember me O Lord, O Lord
Eternal life, eternal life
I want to live eternal life, God save my soul
I want to live eternal life, God save my soul
Boys on to the battlefield
Move on to the battlefield
Move on to the battlefield and fight
Umu Biafra (Biafran citizens)
Move on to the battlefield
Move on to the battlefield
Move on to the battlefield and fight

We shall fight with our machetes and hoes
Our leader, Ojukwu
All the people trust in thee
We shall fight to defend our fatherland
We shall fight with our machetes and hoes
We shall fight to defend Biafra
Our survival depends on this
We shall fight to defend our fatherland

Take my bullet when I die, O Biafra
Take my bullet when I die
Alleluia, give my bullet to someone else
To fight for fatherland

Holy, holy, holy, holy
Odumegwu-Ojukwu
Another saviour

We shall not, we shall not be moved (twice)
Just like a tree that's planted by the water
We shall not be moved,
Ojukwu is behind us
We shall not be moved,
The soldiers are behind us
We shall not be moved
Just like a tree that's planted by the water
We shall not be moved
God is behind us
We shall not be moved
The soldiers are behind us
We shall not be moved
Just like a tree that's planted by the water
We shall not be moved

(Could be repeated several times with the names of other Biafran heroes mentioned repeatedly.)

Songs rendered in Igbo with translations

Umu okoro ibe'm
Jikere kwa nu na heme hem
Umu okoro ibe'm
Jikere kwa nu na heme hem
O le ka unu shi?
Biafra
O le ka unu je?
Biafra
A gam a rapu Biafra

Je Nigeria je biri,
Biafra ga adi ndu,
Nigeria ga nwu ta.

My fellow male comrades
Put on your armour
My fellow male comrades
Put on your armour
Where are you coming from?
Biafra
Where are you going to?
Biafra
I will not leave Biafra
To go and live in Nigeria,
Biafra will survive,
Nigeria will face destruction today.

Enyem Gowon nwa ntinti oge
Amamu ife nge eme ya
Enyem Gowon nwa ntinti oge
Enyem Gowon nwa ntinti oge
Ma agba ya okpa ne-eze
Enyem Gowon nwa ntinti oge
Nna, Nna, Nna, Nna ee, Nna biko
Enyem Gowon nwa ntinti oge

If Gowon is handed over to me briefly
I don't know what I would do to him

If Gowon is handed over to me briefly
If Gowon is handed over to me briefly
I will kick his teeth
If Gowon is handed over to me briefly
God, God, God, God ee, God please
If Gowon is handed over to me briefly

Gowon etiwe,
"Ojukwu, Ojukwu-O, imeriwo
Agam agakwuru Ojukwu e yo ya mbaghara
Ike agwula mu na ami mu-O, imeriwo."

Gowon has shouted,
"Ojukwu, Ojukwu-O you have won
I will go and beg Ojukwu for forgiveness
My troops and I are tired-O, you have won."

Ewo, na mu na nwannem je lu ogu
Akpiri ego, Ifeajuna le nwanne ya
Ewo, na mu na nwannem je lu ogu
Nwannem puta n'uzo le nwanne ya

Ewo, my brothers and I went to battle
Out of greed, Ifeajuna sold his brother
Ewo, my brothers and I went to battle
My brother shamelessly sold his brother

Rapunu anyi-O, rapunu anyi-O ndi Awusa
Okwa unu siri anyi laba
Anyi alaba obodo umunna anyi, ani Biafra
Emesia, emesia unu achuru anyi biaba
Na Chukwu ama kwe
Ebere Chukwu kasi n'uwa
Emesia na anyi ga enwe nmeri-O
Rapunu anyi, rapunu anyi ndi Awusa

Leave us alone, leave us alone you Hausas
It was you who said we should go home
We left to our father's land, land of Biafra
Eventually, eventually you invaded our land
God will not permit it
The mercy of God is supreme in this world
Eventually we will be victorious-O
Leave us alone, leave us alone you Hausas

Nike nike, nike nike
Anyi ga garu ugwu Awusa

With fortitude
We will march to Hausa land

Onye tibe
Tite nwa agwu nu ura (thrice),

Ma mgbe agwu kunitere
Ebelebe egbuo

The person who makes noise
Will wake the baby lion from sleep (thrice)
When the lion wakes up
Tragedy will strike

Aga'm ekwe, aga'm ekwe-o
Aga'm ekwe ma mu gbughi Gowon
Onye Awusa

I will not give up, I will not give up-o
I will not give up until I kill Gowon
Hausa man

Bia nuru olu anyi-o
Nna bia nuru olu anyi-o
Onwe mbge ike Gowon
Ga akari ike Ojukwu
Na bia nuru
Onye kere uwa bia nuru olu anyi-o

Come and hear our voice
Father come and hear our voice
There is no time that Gowon's power

Will surpass Ojukwu's power
Father come and hear
Creator of the world, hear our voice-o

Enyi Biafra le le
Enyi Biafra la la, enyi
Cheta kwanu Aguiyi-Ironsi
Agui-Ironsi bu nwa Biafra
Cheta kwanu Major Nzeogwu
Major Nzeogwu bu nwa Biafra
Cheta kwanu Major Okigbo
Major Okigbo bu nwa Biafra
Cheta kwanu Capt. Archibong
Capt. Archibong bu nwa Biafra
Enyi Biafra le le
Enyi Biafra la la, enyi
Cheta kwanu Okigwe sector
Okigwe sector na ala Biafra
Cheta kwanu Owerri sector
Owerri sector na ala Biafra
Enyi Biafra le le
Enyi Biafra la la, enyi ...

Elephants of Biafra le le
Departed elephants of Biafra, elephants
Remember Aguiyi-Ironsi
Aguiyi-Ironsi is a son of Biafra
Remember Major Nzeogwu

Major Nzeogwu is a son of Biafra
Remember Major Okigbo
Major Okigbo is a son of Biafra
Remember Captain Archibong
Captain Archibong is a son of Biafra
Elephants of Biafra le le
Departed elephants of Biafra, elephants
Remember Okigwe sector
Okigwe sector in the land of Biafra
Remember Owerri sector
Owerri sector in the land of Biafra
Elephants of Biafra le le
Departed elephants of Biafra, elephants ...

Acknowledgements

I am grateful to friends, family members, and acquaintances who assisted me in various ways as I assembled this narrative. My older brother, Charles, offered selfless support each time my memory was vague and needed to be jolted. Peter Millington provided some of the priceless pictures reproduced in the text, as did Ken Conboy and Lieutenant Colonel Francis Archibong (retd.) who kindly supplied images of some Biafran emblems and insignia. (Peter Millington is the son of Regimental Sergeant Major Robert Millington who served in the Nigerian Army Royal Army Ordnance Corps from 1958 to 1962.) Donu Kogbara, daughter of Biafra's High Commissioner in London, Ignatius Kogbara, permitted me to reproduce a unique copy of her father's Biafran passport. I am also indebted to Ekamma Akpan, daughter of the Secretary to the Biafran Government, my uncle Isong Efiong, Angela Ehrlich (Trimnell), Declan O'Connell, and my older sister, Mercy, all of whom furnished me with vital information and pictures. The editorial comments provided by Kerrin Cocks have helped in no small measure to bring out relevant details in various sections of this story.

I owe my strength and confidence to my wife and daughters: Chinwe, Imaeyen, Amaeka, and Idara. Words alone cannot capture their loyalty and matchless love.

Without the security and sustenance of my brothers and sisters I might not be alive today, and certainly would not be able to remember and write. I therefore salute them: Rosalyn Idongesit, Mercy Imoh, Valentine Okon, Charles Asuquo, Francis Mfon, Philippa Aniekanabasi, and Elizabeth Edemma.

At a time when my family was homeless, the generous Trimnells took us in and gave us food, shelter and security under very trying circumstances. The same is true of the Iregbulems who offered us a place to stay after the fall of Umuahia, despite the mounting refugee crisis in their village, Ifakala. These families gave us a reason to be hopeful otherwise I might not have lived to tell this story. I cannot thank them enough.

I am also able to remember and write because of the tireless and sacrificial efforts of those who strived to preserve the lives of millions of Biafrans, offering us renewed hope and restoration. Emmanuel Maurice, an Annang indigene, was only a teenager when he played the risky role of helping to distribute relief supplies across Biafra. Count Carl Gustaf Ericsson von Rosen, a Swedish pilot, flew dangerous relief mission for humanitarian organizations into Biafra. David L Koren was an American volunteer who not only helped to unload humanitarian airlifts that arrived in Biafra, but also helped to evacuate starving children who eventually ended up in São Tomé and Gabon. Jonathan Ambache, a British medical student, died in Biafra while helping to distribute relief supplies to the people. Martin (Marty) Wesson, an American, risked his life performing Public Relations roles and helping to organize airlifts to Biafra. The courageous, relentless, and generous philanthropy of the people of Ireland is a timeless example of Christian compassion. The same is true of the Catholic Church, Caritas International and the Red Cross, without whom Biafra would have wasted away through starvation, sickness, madness, and nakedness. In this regard, Bruce Mayrock also deserves praise. In May 1969 this gallant 20-year-old Columbia University student brought global attention to genocidal crimes against Biafra by immolating himself in front of the United Nations Headquarters in New

York. He is a major reason why I have written this memoir and why I am determined to keep this story alive.

Finally, I am indebted to God, the Higher Power, the Almighty, referred to by different names, for the precious gift of life and creativity.